SUCCESSFUL DINGHY SAILING

David Pitman
and
Steve Ancsell

Illustrations by Alan Batley

First published in 1990
by Sackville Books Ltd
Stradbroke, Suffolk, England

Designed and produced by Sackville Design Group Limited
Art Editor: Rolando Ugolini
Editor: Linda Sonntag

British Library Cataloguing in Publication Data
Pitman, David
Successful Dinghy Sailing. — (Sackville Sports Clinic).
1. Sailing
I. Title

ISBN 0 948615 36 2

Typeset by Jean Cussons, Diss, Norfolk
Reproduced by David Bruce Graphics

Printed and bound in Spain by Graficas Reunidas S.A., Madrid

The authors with to thank Vicky Crabtree for her patient decyphering and keyboard bashing.

Contents

Introduction

Sailing is a superb sport, for young and old alike. It encompasses many disciplines with exciting, exhilarating and sometimes exhausting combinations of wind, water, tactics and strategy. Every time you leave the beach it is a new experience, a test of your ability; and every time you start a race, new tactics come into play. When you reach dry land again there is a warm glow of achievement at having taken on several of the earth's elements. Successful sailing requires a good level of physical fitness, an in-depth understanding of the boat, its sails, mast and controls; and for competition, a knowledge of the racing rules, and a mastery of tactics. Above all it needs common sense ... and this cannot be taught!

This book assumes that the reader understands some of the basic principles of sailing, and explains the interaction of wind and sail, and how sails can be trimmed efficiently for the best performance in all weather conditions. There is advice on how to improve your racing performance, whatever your level of sailing, and, whether you are racing or just cruising, you will find plenty here to enhance your enjoyment. Note that multihull sailing techniques can be very different, and that although there are some tactical manoeuvres in common, many of the boat and sail handling tips in this book may not apply.

CHAPTER ONE

Dinghy Designs

With over two-thirds of the world covered by water providing endless miles of coastline, it is not surprising that boating should be a well developed sport and that a large range of dinghy designs has been established worldwide for many years.

National classes

National classes offer a high degree of competitiveness, and thrive on high levels of ambition. Many believe that winning a World Championship in a popular class is far tougher than winning an Olympic medal — there are always far more competitors, for a start. Because of the various selection systems around the world that elect the national Olympic teams with one boat per class, it is possible that the best competitors may get left out. In the French developed two-man 470 trapeze dinghy, the UK did not select Nigel Buckley and Pete Newlands, the reigning World Champions, for the Seoul Olympics in 1988. This was principally due to a poor performance at a critical selection event.

Each nation has its own favourite dinghy designs and accords them special status. Great Britain has always

UK National Classes

		Loa	H'Cap
Enterprise	**Very popular two man dinghy with chine hull. Ideal first boat for racing or cruising. Main and jib only.**	**4.04**	**118**
Wayfarer	**Strong and ideal for cruising and racing, with two plus crew. Main, jib and spinnaker.**	**4.82**	**116**
G.P. 14	**Introduced as a General Purpose dinghy but now a strong racing fleet. Main, jib and spinnaker.**	**4.27**	**119**
National 12	**Popular, 1950s round-bilged, cold-moulded two man dinghy.**	**3.66**	**117**

been at the forefront of dinghy racing development and can boast many successful designs, which although they do not enjoy International status are well established in many countries. Among these are the blue-sailed Enterprise, the adaptable Wayfarer, and the bell-insignia GP14, all of which are also particularly strong in UK waters. Often boats are designed to suit the particular environment, hence the development of 'wet' boats like the Moth, and 18ft Skiffs from Australia.

International classes

The most successful National classes have become International classes, and are controlled by the world governing body, the International Yacht Racing Union (IYRU). You will find International class dinghies in abundance at almost every sailing club. They enjoy World, and often European Championships every year in addition to their own National Championships. Sailing at this level is intensive, and unless you are well prepared and practised, you will find the competition very tough. Many countries identify the classes that they will support, from children's trainers to the Olympics, and this latter section is usually based on the International range of dinghies.

Olympic classes

The classes sailed at the Olympics are selected from the range of International classes, and they naturally tend to be the most hotly contested. They are successful high-performance dinghies chosen by the IYRU and Olympic committees. A modern Olympic dinghy will feature all the latest technology in hull construction, rig and sail design, and can be very expensive to put on the water; even more so to campaign, as the competition will be on the regatta circuit worldwide.

A good look at a modern Olympic dinghy will give you many clues to how the sails and other equipment are controlled, and how the boat works. Some may be more complicated than others, but all will have common essential equipment. We will analyse these control systems later in the book.

International Classes

		Loa	H'Cap
Optimist	Ideal children's boat, with safety attributes.	2.30	174
Cadet			152
Laser	Strict design makes this popular and successful racing singlehanded worldwide.	4.23	114
420	Two man dinghy with trapeze or similar.	4.20	115
470	Two man dinghy with trapeze or similar.	4.70	103
Contender	Fast trapezing singlehander.		106
Finn	Mens' Olympic singlehander.	4.5	113
505	Two man dinghy with trapeze.	5.05	97
Fireball	Two man trapeze skiff-type dinghy.	4.93	105
14	Twin trapeze, Gennaker.	4.27	97
Europe	The Womens' singlehander for the next Olympics.	3.35	121
Flying Dutchman	Two man dinghy with trapeze and spinnaker — Olympic dinghy.	6.05	94
Moth	Development lightweight singlehander.	3.35	113

Buying your boat

Resist the temptation to rush out and buy a boat until you have spent enough time crewing with more experienced sailors to be sure about committing yourself. You will probably learn the fundamentals of safety, seamanship and racing much more quickly, and be in a better position to train your own crew. Wander into your local sailing club, find the bar and you will be signed up before the day is out. A willing crew who will buy a round is welcome at every club!

When you decide to splash out on a boat, try to identify what you want from your dinghy: cruising or racing, high performance or reliability, speed or relaxation. Remember to consider the practicalities of towing a dinghy around on a trailer, and of storing it at home or at your local sailing club. All these factors will influence your choice of class.

Make sure you take someone who knows about the class when you go off to have a look. Dinghy sailors are always ready to give advice and assistance, so you should not be reluctant to ask. It is a sailor's prerogative, while his feet are on dry land, to divulge his (inevitably) extensive knowledge of any class you care to mention — avoid taking this type on a long journey!

CHAPTER TWO

Where to sail

There is a considerable difference between sailing inland, and on coastal waters, although inland waters, such as reservoirs, lakes and rivers, must be treated with just as much respect as the sea. Reservoirs and larger lakes are not subject to tidal flow, and this makes for easier sailing, especially in windy conditions. Enclosed waters usually mean flatter conditions, so it is easier to manage the boat, and you can concentrate on tuning it for best speed, and on race tactics. With coastal waters, however, winds tend to be stronger, and the influence of tides, and the long distances of 'fetches' between land masses, often add up to rough seas.

Coastal waters

Tides add another dimension to both dinghy racing and cruising. When planning to go sailing, find out exactly when the tide turns, and be aware that a tide with you can take you long distances away from your start point. A thorough knowledge of the local tidal advantages can often make the difference between winning and losing a race. Always watch the local experts, who will often take off in what seems an illogical direction: there is usually a very good reason behind it.

Another way to gain advantage when racing is to identify the direction and strength of the tide at different points on the course. One of the reasons why successful sailors leave early for the race is so that they can sail to one, or several of the marks and find out what is happening there. An apple core makes the perfect marker, and by dropping it at a mark, then sailing around it for 30 seconds or so, you can see how strong the current is, and by using the compass, identify its direction. This will enable you to decide on your strategy for the race.

•**Tip** Some lakes and all rivers have currents, so watch out for drift by taking a bearing or transit (see p.77) when motionless in the water.

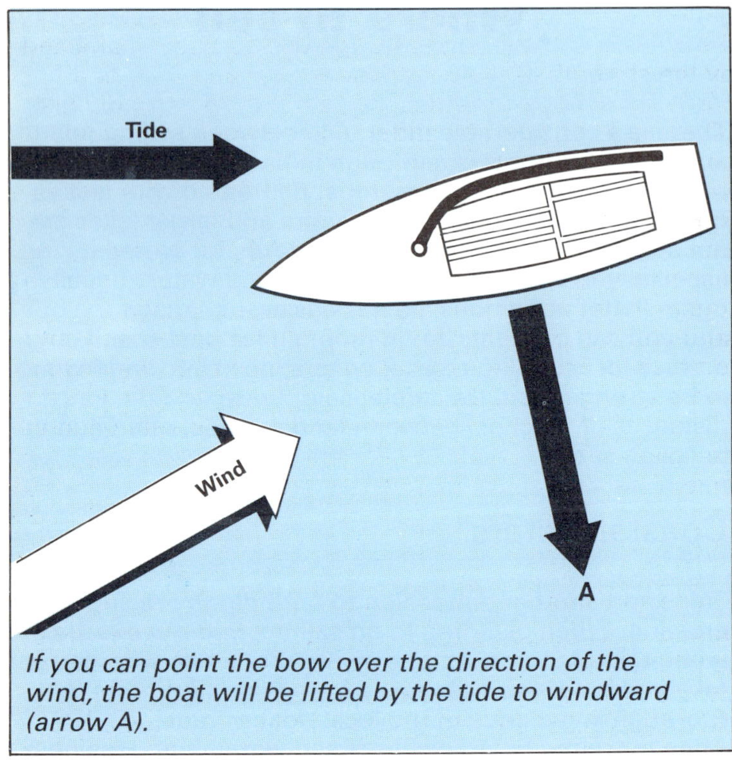

If you can point the bow over the direction of the wind, the boat will be lifted by the tide to windward (arrow A).

Tide and wind

The effect of wind on tide can be quite frightening in some circumstances, and it is important to know exactly where the tides run strong. When the wind blows in the same direction as the tide it tends to create a flattening effect on the surface of the water. When the tide turns, an experienced sailor will notice the difference in the wave

•**Tip** The 'lee-bow' effect (p.71) is probably one of the biggest advantages that you can gain over competitors who have not identified it. When sailing into a tide, particularly a strong one, if you can get the direction of your dinghy above the direction of tide so that it passes on your leeward bow, then you will effectively be pushed to windward. This might mean 'pinching' into the wind, and losing some boatspeed, but the rewards can be great.

pattern within a few minutes of the change. The height of the wave and depth of the trough will be directly affected by the strength of the wind, and the speed of the tidal currents. Usually currents tend to run more strongly just off exposed headlands, and the difference in surface conditions is quite marked.

Spring and neap tides
The gravitational effects of the sun and moon on the earth's seas create tides. When both sun and moon act together, much stronger tides are created, known as spring tides. These can be identified from a tide table by increased height and a greater difference between high and low, which creates much stronger currents.

Neap tides, when sun and moon are in opposition, are the lowest in the cycle, and here tidal differences are much less, and currents much weaker.

Inland waters

Inland sailing changes the concentration from currents on to windshifts. Buildings or land features such as trees can twist and change the direction of the wind. These wind twists (see p.35) are increasingly important when other factors, like tide, are removed.

The experienced sailor will probably change his rig settings when sailing inland. With calmer water, sails can be set flatter for the same wind strength, as the boat does not need so much power to sail through waves. Remember also that inland sailing can often go ahead when racing on the coast would normally be cancelled because of strong winds, wave conditions, and other safety considerations. The responsibility of deciding whether to sail or not is on you, and sometimes it is safer and more sensible to get ashore without damaging sails and equipment. Try to be aware of your experience, and be prepared to come ashore if things are getting wild. Sailors from clubs along the coastline are likely to be already sitting in the bar!

CHAPTER THREE

Planning ahead

Every time you leave the shore the trip should be planned — and always for the worst possible eventuality. Sailing is a sport that has to take the natural elements of wind and tides into account, and a rig failure once afloat can lead to a potentially serious situation.

Factors to take into account

Weather

Always check the local weather so that you can plan for both too much and too little wind. When racing you will want to know if the wind is likely to back or veer during the race, and position yourself accordingly.

Tides

Find out the state of the tides or currents in the area you are sailing, and when they change direction.

Safety

If you are competing it is usual to have rescue boats around, but if you are in transit or cruising you will need additional precautions, such as taking an anchor and suitable attire, paddle, spare ropes for a tow, and money for a phone call, and a beer. Always tell someone your plans before leaving, and call them if they change; otherwise expect to find an irate helicopter pilot overhead! A chat to the rescue facilities will highlight common local problems with dinghy sailing, like going afloat without sufficient protection from the water and cold; and a chat in the changing rooms with your competitors will emphasize what you should not forget to take with you.

A compass is often essential, along with a countdown watch or timer. These things are no use in your kit bag on the shore. Sailing instructions are also an essential part of a racing sailor's equipment, even though they might end up as soggy papier-mâché in your pocket. Do not forget other essential equipment, like trapeze belts, and even more importantly, make sure the drain bungs are secured before launching — even good sailors have started races half full of water at some stage in their lives!

CHAPTER FOUR

Aerofoils and the wind

The airflow across the sails creates the force that drives the dinghy along, so in order to get the best from your sails, you need to understand the basic principles of airflow. Always think of your sails as a total aerofoil or wing, and immediately you will recognize the importance of each sail working in unison with the rest. Aerofoils can be powerful, depending on their depth, and width of section. A jumbo jet is held in the sky by exactly the same principles of physics that drive sailing boats.

When an aerofoil is working correctly air flows smoothly over both surfaces. It is important to identify 'attached' clean flow with the use of tell-tales (p.21). Air flowing over the upper curve is accelerated, creating a lower pressure area than on the lower surface. The higher pressure air tries to fill the lower, and the resultant force represents 'lift'.

This difference in pressure generates the power in the total aerofoil. This can be increased or decreased by making the sailplan sections fuller or flatter, depending on

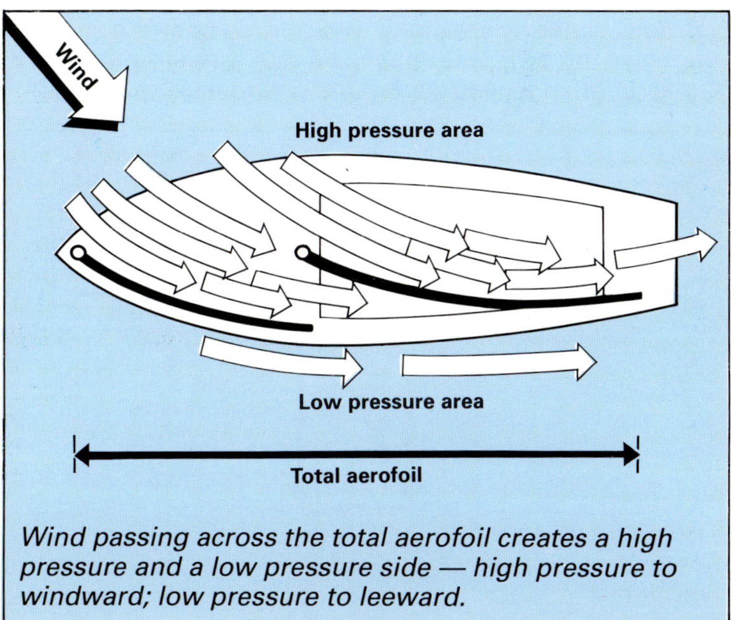

Wind passing across the total aerofoil creates a high pressure and a low pressure side — high pressure to windward; low pressure to leeward.

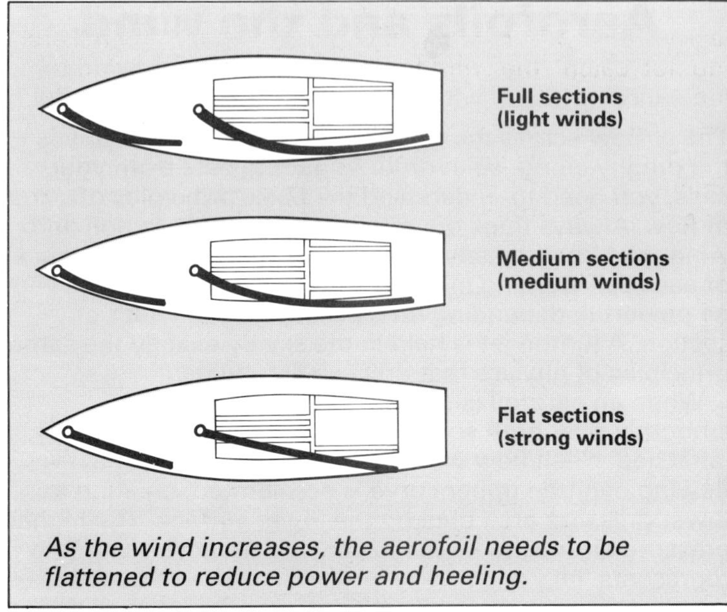

As the wind increases, the aerofoil needs to be flattened to reduce power and heeling.

the windspeed. This is how flaps work on aircraft wings, moving to increase the curve (camber) when slowing down for landing, while maintaining the same lift. Sail aerofoils similarly create lift, which on a boat is a sideways force. This is converted into forward motion by the addition of a centreboard, or keel in a yacht.

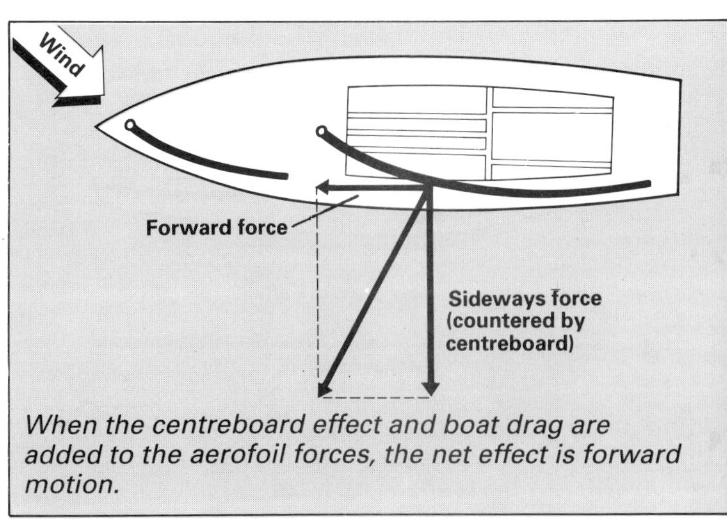

When the centreboard effect and boat drag are added to the aerofoil forces, the net effect is forward motion.

Sails will always work more efficiently with airflow across them, even when sailing down wind. Spinnakers do not 'catch' the wind for instance, but allow wind to flow through them with the deepest and most powerful aerofoil sections giving lift and speed.

When the sails are in stall, often when over-sheeted relative to the direction sailed, the obvious result is slow speed — catastrophic when it happens to an aeroplane!

Wind always flows through spinnakers. When running (above), the wind usually enters at the top and exhausts at the bottom, giving the sail lift. When reaching (right), the airflow is across the sail, exhausting from the leech.

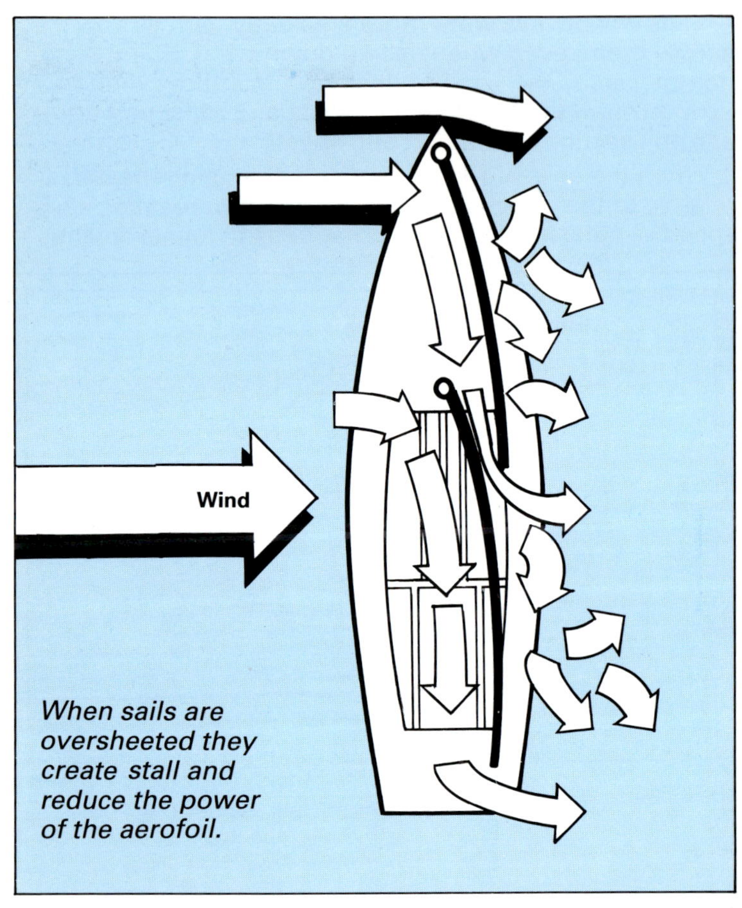

When sails are oversheeted they create stall and reduce the power of the aerofoil.

The slot effect

Bermudan sailplans (mainsail, and jib or genoa) are very efficient at relatively low speeds because they create a slot effect between the two sails. Just like an aeroplane's wing on take-off, slots and flaps are used to increase the general depth of aerofoil, and to guide and accelerate the air on to the main foil of the wing, or in our case, the mainsail. For best performance the slot between the jib and mainsail must not be too small, or 'closed', otherwise the airflow is 'choked'. On the other hand, if it is too open, the aerofoil loses power. To get the exact inboard lateral position for sheeting the slot correctly, watch experienced

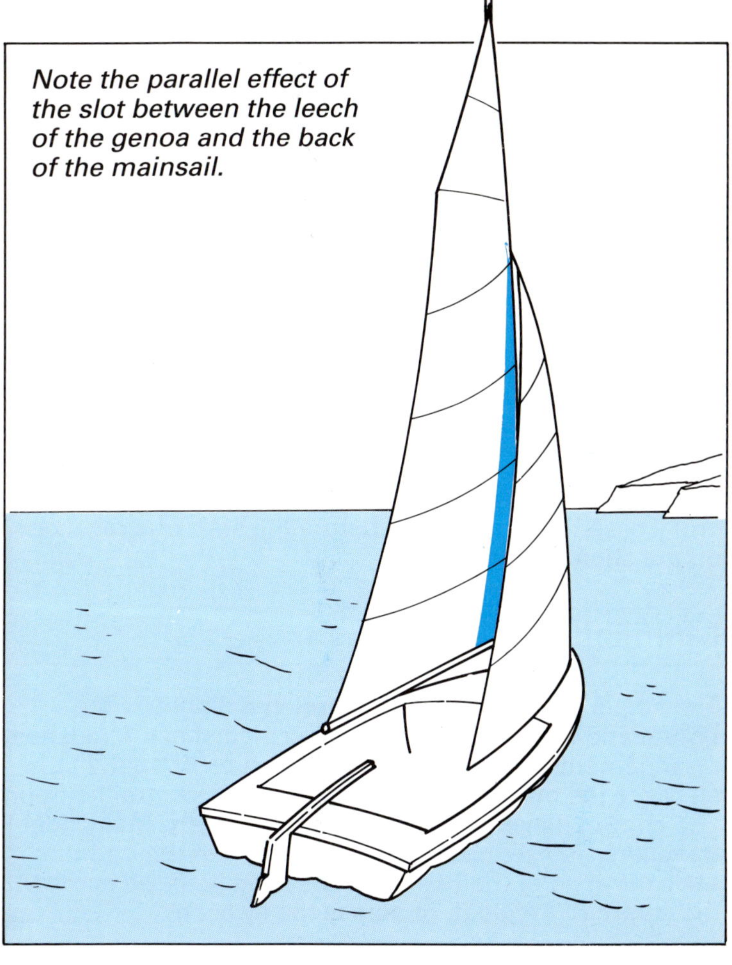

Note the parallel effect of the slot between the leech of the genoa and the back of the mainsail.

sailors in your class, as they will have spent much time testing every position possible.

The jib leech should be set approximately parallel to the leeward side of the mainsail. Stand well away from the rig after setting it up on the shore,and look at it from the leeward quarter. As the wind increases in speed the jib leech should be opened, otherwise it will back wind the mainsail. Open the leech by moving the sheet lead aft and outboard, or raking the mast more aft.

Many dinghies have camber lines across both mainsail and jib from luff to leech. These are simply pen or tape lines to help show how full or flat the sails are to the crew's eyes.

CHAPTER FIVE

Sails and shapes

Modern sails are very different from those made even a few seasons ago. There have been considerable advances in sailcloth technology, and this, coupled with computer-aided designs, means stronger, more stable sails. Often described under their trade names Terylene© and Dacron©, sailcloths are finished with resin coatings to stabilize the cloth and reduce stretch. Other new plastic-coated materials, such as Mylar ©, are increasing in popularity, because of their strength, stability and reduced weight.

Take care not to crease the sails when putting them away after the day's sailing, or let them flap unnecessarily, for example before the start of a race, or on the shore.

Mainsail

The single most important control in a dinghy is the boom, and this is controlled by the mainsheet. Mainsheet arrangement varies according to the type of boat, but in all cases the mainsheet should be able to centre the boom and control its vertical movement accurately. Mainsheet travellers also set up the sheeting angle of the boom to the centreline of the boat, and they can be fitted across the centre of the boat, or across the transom.

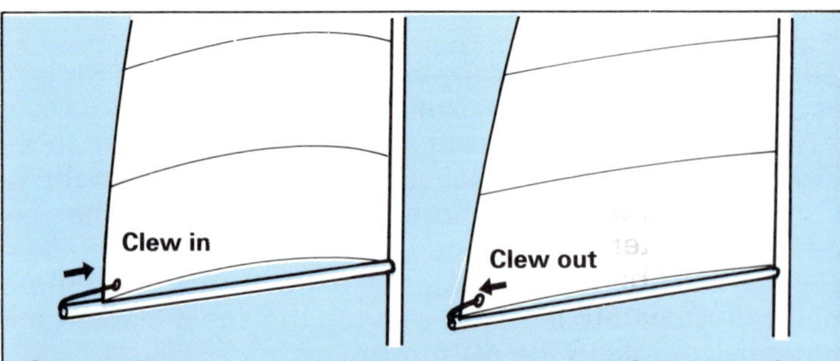

Clew adjustment can change the overall fullness of the sail. Clew in (left), makes a deeper, more powerful sail; clew out to maximum (right), gives a flatter, less powerful effect.

For all classes, the traveller control centres the boom in light to medium winds, until the dinghy becomes overpowered. When all other sail flattening methods have been employed to reduce the fullness in the sail, and power in the rig, then the traveller is set progressively to leeward, away from the centreline. This reduces pointing ability but makes the boat more manageable, and probably faster.

The clew of the mainsail is the next most important control, as it dramatically changes the shape of the aerofoil, and therefore the power in the sail. An accurate adjustment is needed here because an inch (2.5cm) either way will make a big difference to the shape.

As soon as the boat begins to heel and the sails become too powerful, then the clew position needs to be adjusted aft. In strong winds pull it out as far as it will go (or is allowed in class rules) to flatten the sail.

Cunningham control

Over the past few seasons, sailors have become confused about the use of the Cunningham sail control. Originally, its purpose was to remove wrinkles that appear down the front (luff) of the sail when beating to windward. It tidied up the sail and made the shape more even. But, nowadays, in many two-handed classes, the Cunningham control is left off when beating, to keep the forward part of the sail soft. This does not look good, but it allows for more fullness in the front of the sail, and prevents airflow through the slot between jib leech and mainsail from becoming 'choked'. Other classes still use the Cunningham control to flatten the sail, and to open the leech in strong winds.

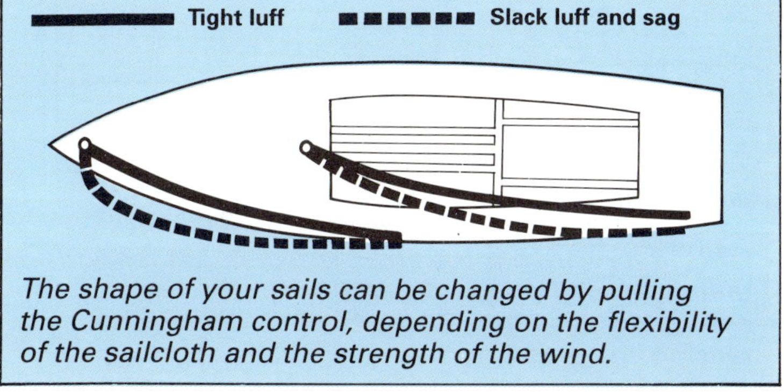

The shape of your sails can be changed by pulling the Cunningham control, depending on the flexibility of the sailcloth and the strength of the wind.

•Tip Watch out for stretch in both the main and jib halyards. After sailing for a short while, they will stretch. Sail tuning can get confusing if the mainsail comes down the luff a few inches. On the jib or genoa this is much more serious, because it will allow the luff of the sail to sag to leeward.

By pulling really hard on the Cunningham, you will put a lot of tension in the sailcloth up the luff, which will slightly distort the material. This has the effect of opening the leech near the top, thus reducing pressure in the sail.

Jib and genoa

In order to get the best sheeting position, some dinghies are fitted with a fore and aft adjustment, or track. This enables the correct position to be selected for different wind, or mast rake conditions.

With the sheet block in the correct position, the luff of

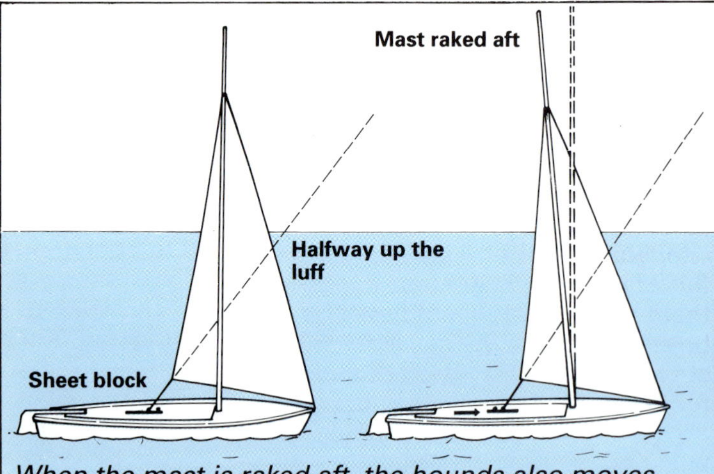

When the mast is raked aft, the hounds also moves aft, and the genoa sheet position will have to be adjusted. Without any rig changes, moving the fairlead forward has the effect of increasing tension on the leech of the genoa, and vice versa. For stronger winds move fairleads aft to reduce leech tension and pressure.

the jib will break (or flutter) evenly from top to bottom when you point up into the wind. The sheet block can then be set farther aft to open the upper jib leech for stronger winds, or slightly farther forward to tighten the leech, if required. Do not forget, however, that if the mast rake is increased, then both the jib sheet leads will need to be adjusted, because the whole jib changes position.

When the jib or genoa is set up, it is worth looking at how the shape changes with increasing tension in the sheet. There is often a considerable difference in sail shape between firm sheeting and very hard sheeting, and it is necessary for the crew to be aware of the difference. When the wind falls away a little the crew should ease the sheet slightly, to give the jib more fullness and power. A marker on each sheet where it passes next to the fairlead is essential for accurate control.

Use of tell-tales

If attached in the right place, a tell-tale is both an indicator of apparent wind direction and a clue to how the wind is flowing over the sails. It enables you to correct direction, or sail setting. Tell-tales can be lengths of coloured wool, or strips of nylon, or even magnetic tape from a cassette. They should be positioned where they can be seen, and where the flow is normally stable.

It is usual to have several tell-tales spaced down either side of the luff on a jib or genoa, and about 9 inches (23cm) from the boltrope at the front. When sailing to windward, the tell-tale on the windward side will lift and flutter if you sail too close to the wind, indicating that there is a breakdown of flow. If the leeward tell-tale can be seen through the sailcloth, you will notice it flutter and stall if you sail too far off the wind, or if the jib is too tight for the wind direction. In this way the tell-tales can be an accurate guide to sail setting and direction, especially when sailing to windward.

Tell-tales are often also fitted to the upper leech of mainsails, and in this position they will indicate if the leech of the sail is set correctly for the wind strength. If all the tell-tales are flowing off the back of the leech, then the air flow is working well across the sails. If, however, the tell-tales are in stall, then the sail is too tight, or too close to the centreline. Fast sailors do let the very top tell-tale

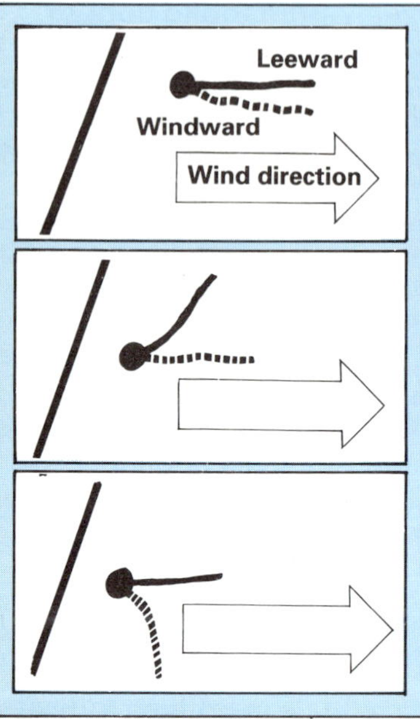

Sailing to windward correctly, the windward telltale should be flying straight, with the leeward telltale just in stall.

Windward side telltale lifts and flutters when too close to the wind (stall). Leeward side still flies.

Leeward side telltale drops when the sail is oversheeted (stall).

(usually set at the end of the top batten) stall and flutter to get the best power and performance to windward, although all the other tales must be flowing.

Spinnaker

Spinnakers are always best set with their clews level (when the boat is not heeled). As the wind gets stronger, the spinnaker will want to fly higher, and the pole height will need constantly to be adjusted. By keeping the clews level, the distortion of shape is reduced across the sail. Think of the spinnaker as a very big, full genoa. The tack is set on the end of the spinnaker pole and so the tack position can be adjusted up and down, and fore and aft. This sail, more than any other, is really flexible.

Just as you need to keep the luff of the main or jib at the front of the aerofoil, the spinnaker luff should be trimmed backwards, aft, into the wind to get the best setting.

When the pole is trimmed aft (into the wind) as far as possible, the crew should trim the spinnaker so that the luff is just curling. The spinnaker should be trimmed continuously and set like this for the whole leg.

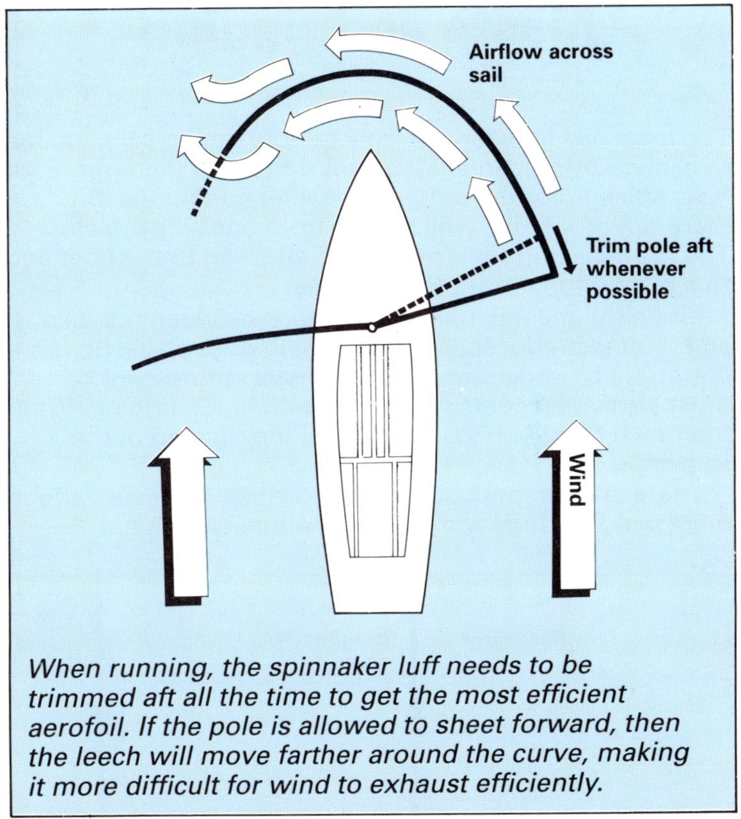

When running, the spinnaker luff needs to be trimmed aft all the time to get the most efficient aerofoil. If the pole is allowed to sheet forward, then the leech will move farther around the curve, making it more difficult for wind to exhaust efficiently.

In addition to spinnaker guy adjustment (pole aft) the pole has to be adjusted for height. As the windspeed increases, it will tend to blow the spinnaker higher. Keep adjusting the pole up and down, so that the spinnaker can fly at the right height. When the boat is level and upright, so the two clews should be also. When the wind gets light, it is easy to forget to lower the pole, and the spinnaker will collapse more easily.

Each different type of dinghy has its own method of spinnaker launching and recovery, but whatever method, it is important to practise for speed and efficiency. Once the spinnaker is set, the dinghy usually becomes much more steady even in heavy winds, because of the vertical lift from the spinnaker. Success stems from being able to judge how long to keep it up, and getting it stowed away fast, and in time for a controlled mark rounding. Practice is the only answer.

CHAPTER SIX

Masts and rigging

The mast can be used not only to hold up the sailplan, but to change the section in the sails and make them more, or less, efficient for the ambient weather conditions. But there are problems, which stem from one single factor. The mast is controlled by rigging attached to the boat and to a plate on the mast, the 'hounds'.

When the mast bends, the distance between the deck and hounds reduces, and the rigging goes slack. So it is important to understand that the mast stiffness, or bend, must always be controlled by tension in the rigging. With too much bend you lose control of the rig, and of the sailshape.

There are two opposing demands here because various mast bend settings will change the mainsail shape

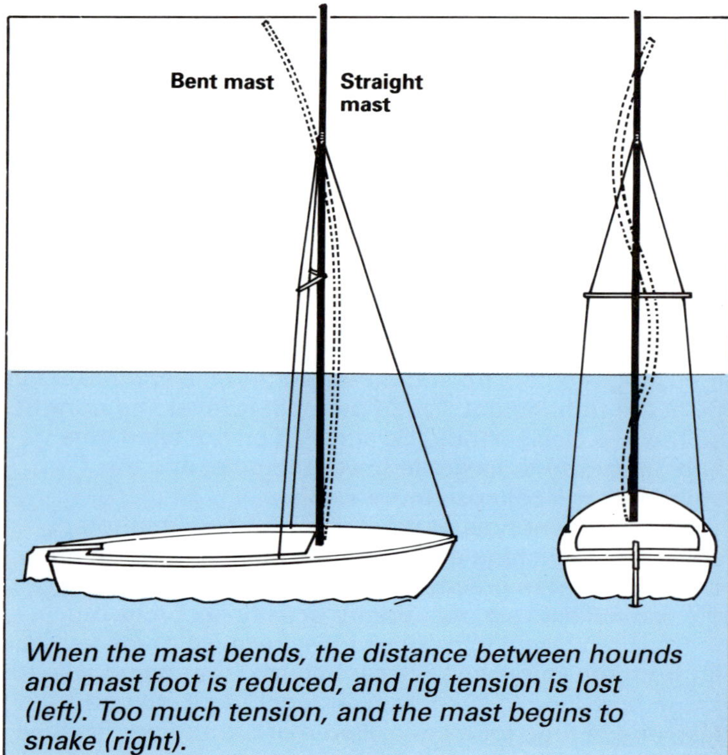

When the mast bends, the distance between hounds and mast foot is reduced, and rig tension is lost (left). Too much tension, and the mast begins to snake (right).

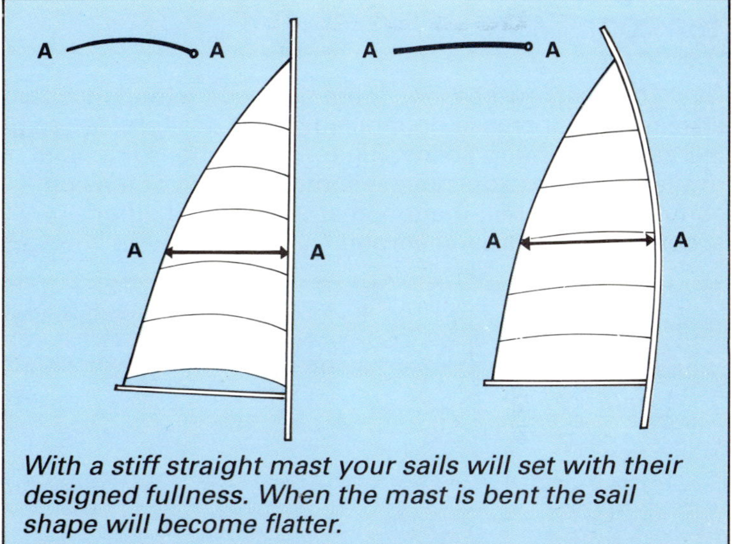

With a stiff straight mast your sails will set with their designed fullness. When the mast is bent the sail shape will become flatter.

dependent on wind conditions. However, slackness in the rig will allow the forestay, and therefore the jib luff, to sag, reducing pointing ability. If too much rig tension is used to remove sag, then it can create compression bending, which again is detrimental to the rig, and to the boat.

The mast can usually be controlled by careful adjustment to the spreaders. When they are offset forward and outwards, they have the effect of stiffening the mast against the direction of bend.

Each class has developed the best settings for tension and angle of deflection and this information is often available from builders, sailmakers or class associations.

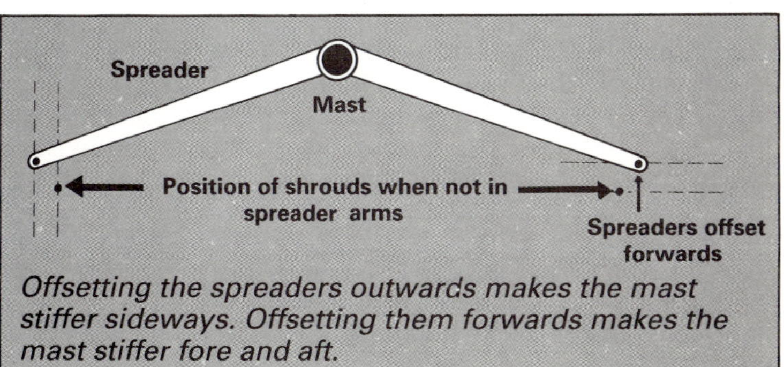

Offsetting the spreaders outwards makes the mast stiffer sideways. Offsetting them forwards makes the mast stiffer fore and aft.

Tension

Over the past few seasons there has been a tendency for all classes to increase rig tension to remove forestay sag, increasing pointing ability. Rig tension gauges are now available so that you can get some measure of tension control. Remember, though, that tension will differ according to the size of shroud.

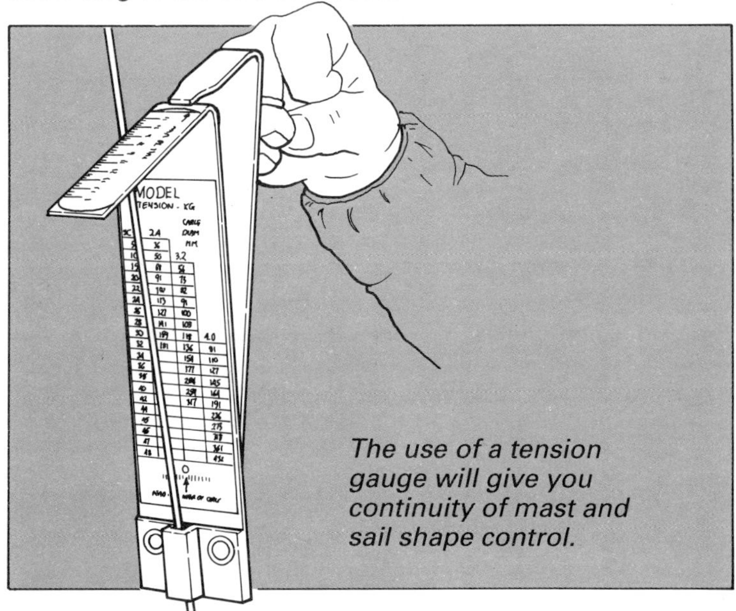

The use of a tension gauge will give you continuity of mast and sail shape control.

Mast rake

It is very unusual for a mast to be fitted upright in a boat, and it certainly looks wrong. Masts are raked (heeled) aft, to improve the balance of the boat, and to assist with 'tuning'. Windward performance can be improved by increasing the rake. The more it blows, the more the rig should be raked for best performance.

It is also known that for downwind sailing, rake is a disadvantage, and the mast is best positioned upright, or even forward, towards the bow; so getting the best setting for both upwind and downwind sailing is a headache, and a balance can be achieved only by experiment.

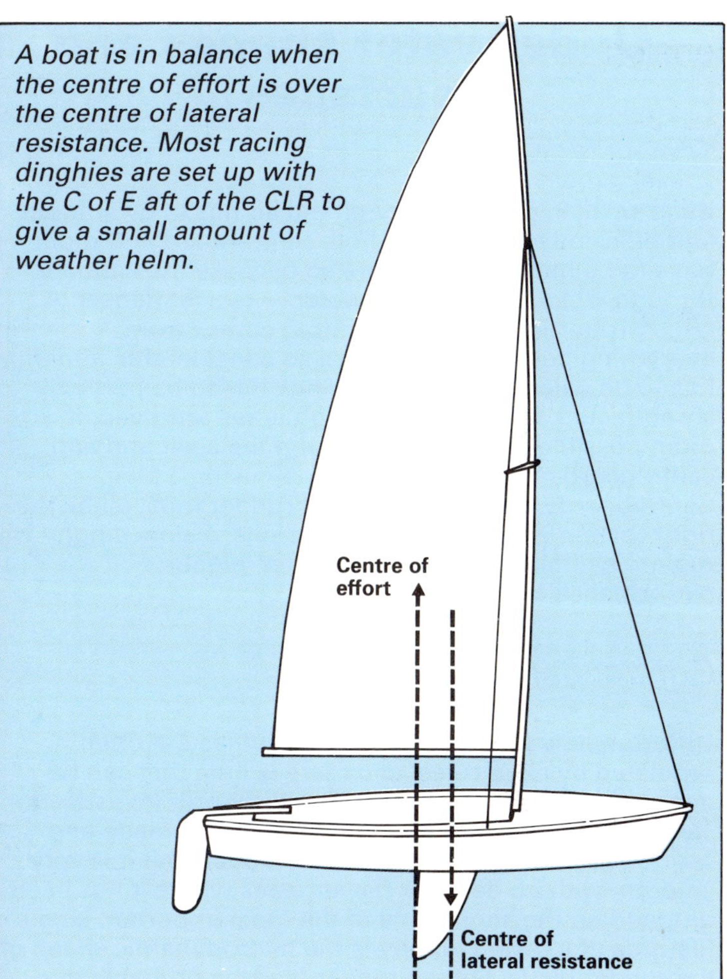

A boat is in balance when the centre of effort is over the centre of lateral resistance. Most racing dinghies are set up with the C of E aft of the CLR to give a small amount of weather helm.

Calibration

With your rig under load it is important that everything should be calibrated, and written down, so that you are able to reproduce the exact settings and tension. If you fail to do this, you will be travelling to regatta after regatta with no continuity of rig or sail settings, and although you might get lucky once, it is unlikely that you will do it again! Mark *every* adjustment with a calibrated strip and note down positions and tension.

CHAPTER SEVEN

Underwater shapes and surfaces

If the sailplan passing through the air has to be smooth and efficiently shaped, the hull, centreboard and rudder have to be meticulously more so because the element through which they pass — water — is a lot denser. A large proportion of the boat's drag comes from everything below the waterline, so considerable attention has to be paid to this area. The hull has to be perfectly smooth, and any bumps or rough areas removed. It is often possible to smooth in around the keelband and centreboard or daggerboard box by using a filler. Centreboards, daggerboards and rudder must all be the right section and, as with sail aerofoils, a slow dinghy will require a different section to a faster, higher performance craft.

Centreboards and rudders

Unfortunately these sections and profiles are often regulated by class rules, and there is little that can be done to improve their shape. But it is worth investigation. Take a look at the class Champion's rudder blade and centreboard and you will probably notice that it is very smooth, with no dents or flat surfaces where it has been dragged up the shore. One of the most important single features of a racing dinghy is the hydrodynamic shape of the rudder blade, yet the rudder blade is probably the most abused piece of equipment on the boat. It costs very little to buy a protective bag for it, so why not give it a treat!

Keeping the boat flat

Your hull is likely to present its most efficient underwater shape when the boat is upright. As heel increases, a variety of unwanted factors come into force: the centreboard and rudder become less efficient; the sails begin to spill air out of the top. The hull shape becomes less efficient as it rides on its quarter. Worst of all, increased weather helm is created, because the rudder is

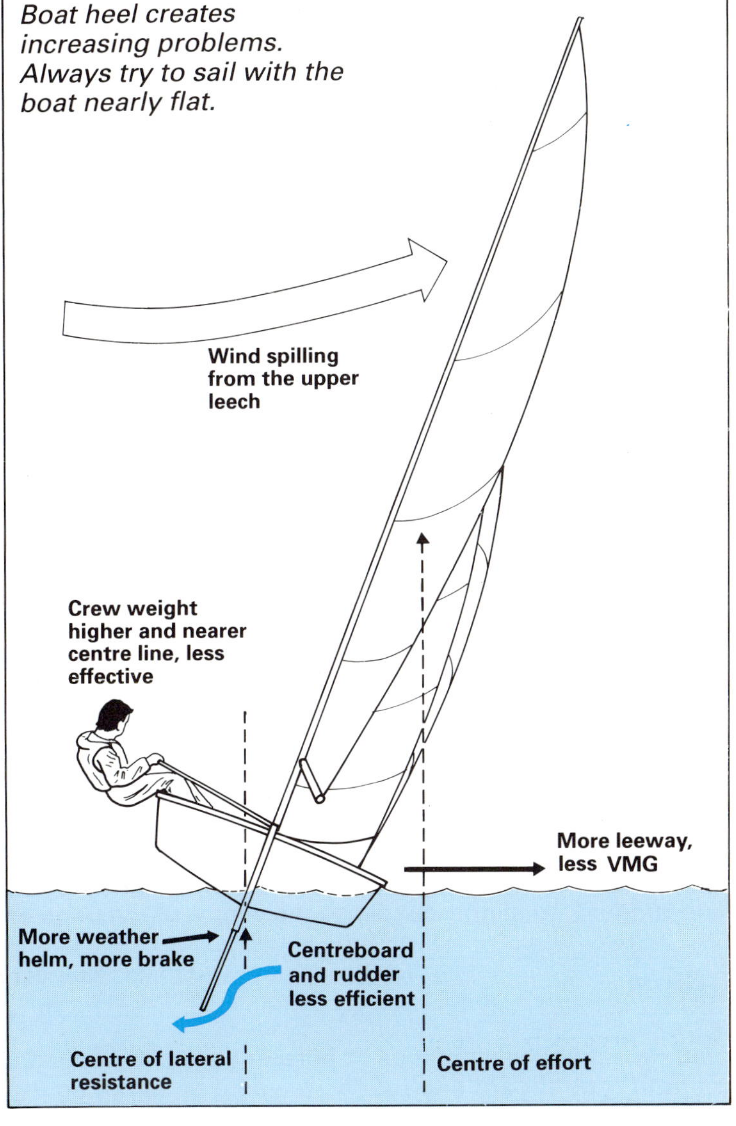

effectively lifted away from the centreline of effort; more leverage is required to keep the boat on course, and this naturally slows the boat.

As the boat heels, it slides increasingly sideways (makes leeway) and you rapidly lose distance to windward. As heel increases, then the crew weight becomes less efficient and so wind has to be spilled from the sails. All this means that constant concentration is needed to keep the boat flat!

Cavitation

When you venture out in stronger winds, make sure you give the rudder a good test by forcing the boat to broach, especially when reaching. This creates a lot of force on the rudder blade. What can happen with a badly shaped rudder, or a wrongly pivoted rudder, is that the water flow breaks down, creating a vacuum along one side, sucking air down from the surface, and resulting in the unmistakable sound of cavitation and subsequent reduced control.

The first effect the helmsman will feel is a sudden loss of steering, and this is just what you want to avoid along the first reach of a race with lots of other — expensive — boats around you!

Weed

Most rudders and centreboards are painted white, so that you can more easily detect weed and plastic bags that often catch on the foils. It is always difficult to decide whether to slow down to get rid of weed; it is almost always worth it. Whenever you feel that the boat is not going as fast as usual, get your head over the side and check. There is usually so much going on above the water that you forget about weed until it is much too late!

Try to remove any sideways slack in the centreboard box by fitting 'fillers' to the board. Putting washers on the pivot bolt is one way of doing it. This will make the board more efficient, and probably help bring the centreboard and rudder into alignment along the centre of the boat.

Edges

Trailing edges are almost as important as leading edges on both centreboard and rudder. It would be tempting to

> •**Tip** A 'singing' vibration from either rudder or centreboard indicates that you are going fast, and that the rudder sections may not be uniform on each side. Look carefully at the trailing edge, which may need reshaping.

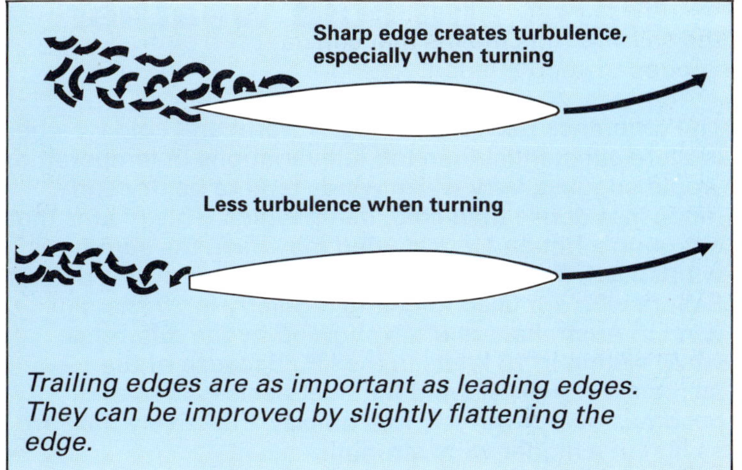

Trailing edges are as important as leading edges. They can be improved by slightly flattening the edge.

think that the sharper the trailing edge, the better the flow around it, but it does seem that water flows more cleanly past a sharp corner, than round a razor-sharp trailing edge. Often vibration can be caused in either the centreboard or the rudder when leading or trailing edges are not correct, or the sections are uneven or different from one side to the other.

The edge between hull and transom should also be sharp, as this will improve the waterflow, especially when planing at speed.

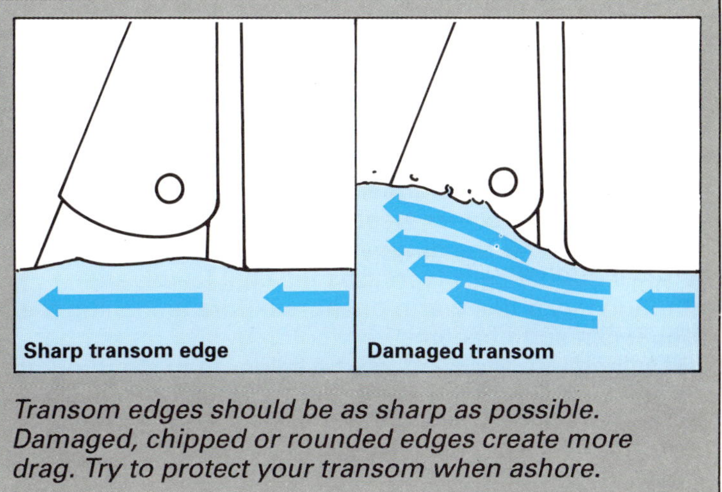

Transom edges should be as sharp as possible. Damaged, chipped or rounded edges create more drag. Try to protect your transom when ashore.

CHAPTER EIGHT

Warm and cold weather

The difference between sailing in warm and cold weather is more substantial than the felt variations in temperature would suggest. Very warm winds tend to be dry and much less dense than cold, damp winds. This means that although a hot and a cold wind may have the same windspeed, the cold wind will feel stronger or heavier. Sailors who are used to racing regularly in 25 knots of wind in Australia, are often shocked by the difference when sailing in 25 knots in the UK. Because of the increased weight of wind the boat heels earlier, and becomes overpowered more quickly. Effectively they are sailing in a higher wind strength.

Ideally, wind strength would not be measured by windspeed, as with the still widely used, and arbitrary, Beaufort Scale of 1 to 12 (p.80), or indeed the more modern knots or metres per second. The best way to describe a wind condition would be to measure its actual pressure. Sailmakers would welcome a revised system of measurement with open arms. In the world of top yacht racing, the variety of foresails available to the crew is extensive, sizes and shapes being chosen according to wind strength. But the only current method of measuring what a sail will cope with is through apparent windspeed from instrumentation.

Development of sail shapes will often be different around the world, even though the class of dinghy may be the same. Local sailmakers will develop the best possible design, with the most powerful shape for the local conditions. If winds tend to be cold and wet, the sails will be flatter. Conversely, in hot sunny climates, they will be very much fuller.

The change to colder weather brings another factor into consideration for the dinghy sailor. A drop of a few degrees dramatically increases the chill factor, and although it can feel warm onshore before launching the boat, it can soon become very cold. Always remember that sailing into the wind will be colder than standing on the beach. It is better to take clothes off when you are hot, rather than go unprotected and get really cold.

If you are not used to sailing in hot and sunny weather, always consider protecting your head from too much sun.

CHAPTER NINE

Wind effects

The very first thing that a racing dinghy sailor must learn about the wind is that its direction is very seldom stable.

Shifts

When cruising or relaxing you are unlikely to be aware of anything but the most severe of windshifts (changes in direction). However, it pays to take note of all windshifts, minor as well as major, even when cruising, if time is not with you. The wind is constantly fluctuating, like the waves at sea, and even small changes in direction can help or hinder in a big way.

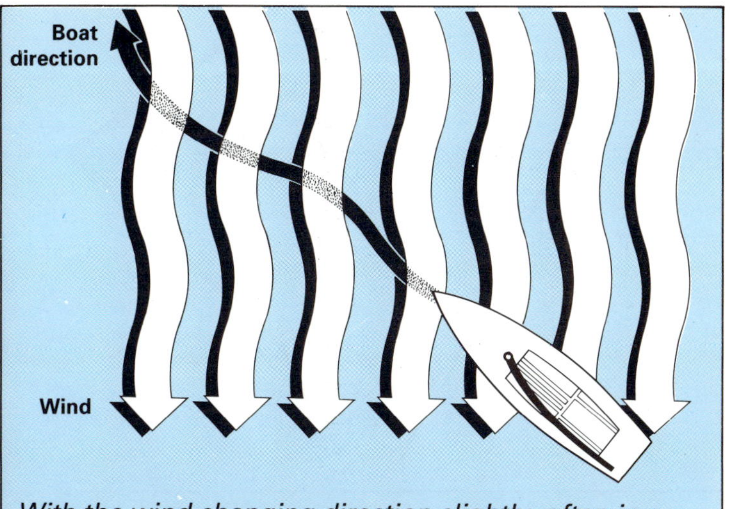

With the wind changing direction slightly, often in a regular cycle, the boat's heading will also change if you sail close hauled.

When sailing through windshifts, the direction of the boat will change slightly. This has the effect of either shortening or lengthening the distance to be sailed to the windward mark. By always sailing on the tack that gets you closer to the mark, you can reduce the distance considerably over a rival who sails on the wrong shifts.

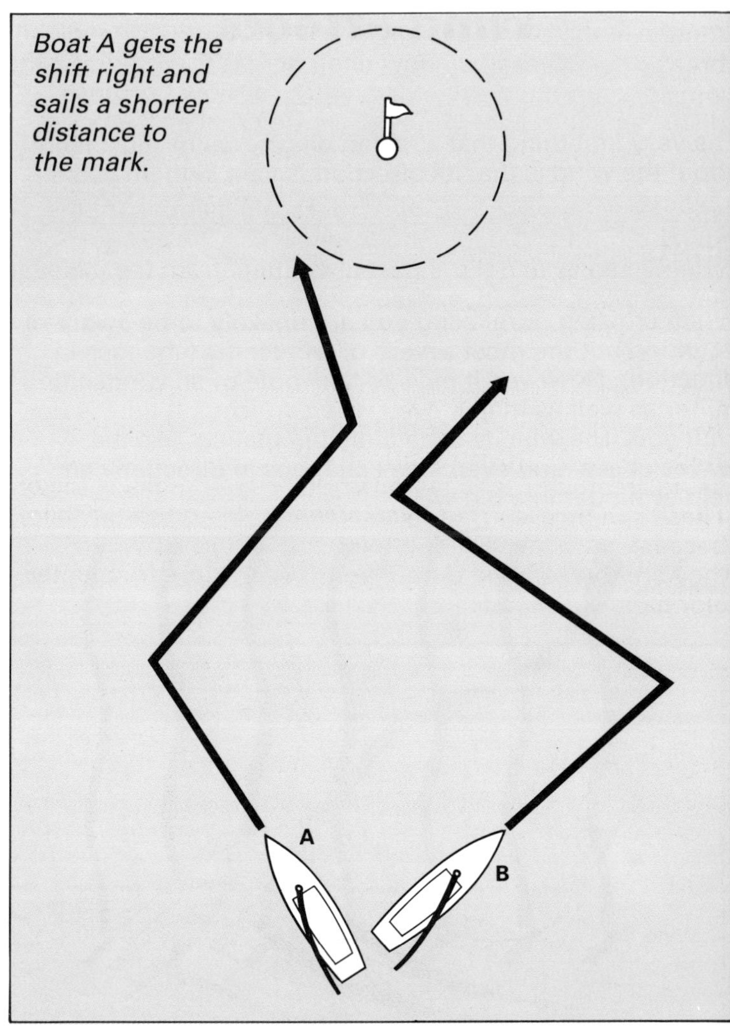

To take advantage of windshifts, you must first identify them. The only way to achieve this is with a good clear-reading compass with efficient damping. Shift work is something to be practised at every opportunity, and you will rapidly get a feel for the type and degree of shifts if you start logging them from the moment you get on or near the course. Well sailed boats will often be covered with chinagraph pencil marks, where the helmsman has recorded compass direction every few minutes so as to identify the changing wind pattern.

Windshifts and clouds
Clouds in the sky, especially low level cumulus cloud, will break down the steady flow of air across the water. As the wind pushes the cloud along, so the airflow becomes disturbed, and other temperature difference effects are experienced. This can cause very gusty conditions below and in front, but it is often a normal pattern, so can be predicted. Because you can expect this 'fanning' of the wind in front of bigger clouds, always try to position yourself so as to get the best advantage from the possible 'lift' on port or starboard tack.

Twists

Twists in the wind are similar to shifts but are more stable, and happen regularly in a particular place, often being created by a headland or other geographical factor. These can be even more valuable to the successful sailor because once identified, often by reference to a chart; they are there all the time. Twists occur more frequently along the coastlines.

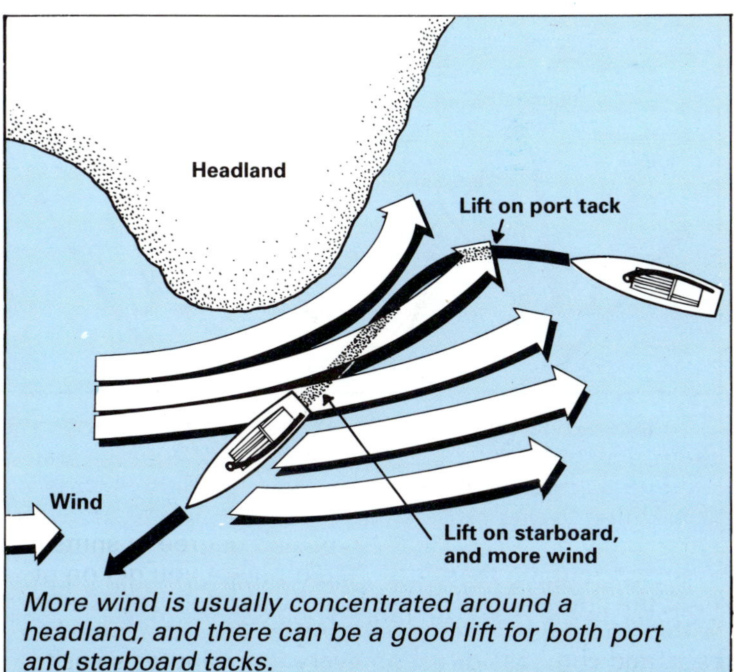

More wind is usually concentrated around a headland, and there can be a good lift for both port and starboard tacks.

> **•Tip** The wind always veers off its normal direction towards the perpendicular when it crosses the coastline.

'Lifts' and 'knocks'

The wind fluctuates regularly, and by recording the compass reading of the dinghy, when sailing consistently to windward, the pattern can be identified. If the wind 'lifts' the bow of the boat towards the mark 5 degrees or more, do *not* tack, but stay with it. If the reverse happens and the bow is 'knocked' 5 degrees, there is an advantage in tacking. However, care must be taken in balancing the number of tacks against the windshift advantage. It is no good tacking all over the ocean on every few degrees of change!

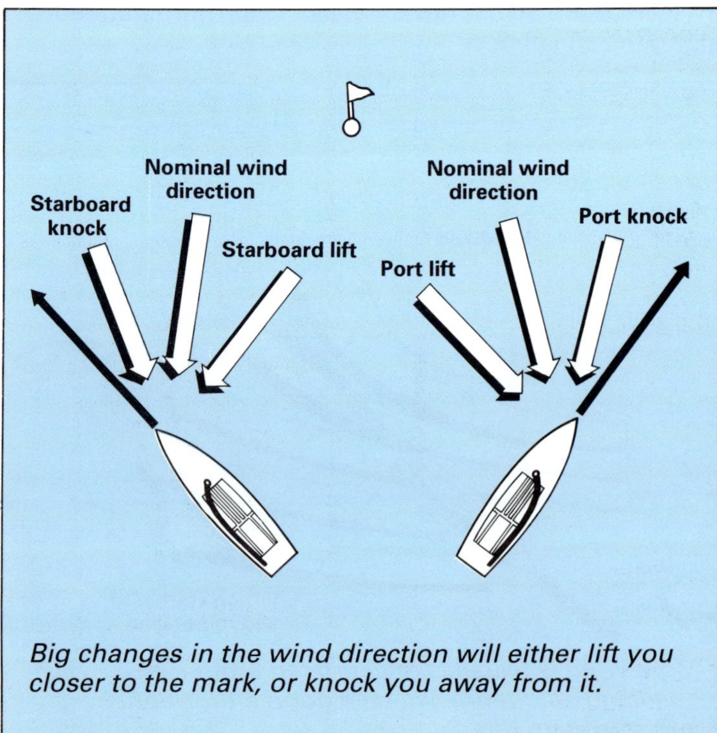

Big changes in the wind direction will either lift you closer to the mark, or knock you away from it.

•**Tip** Remember, when using the compass reading for the direction of the boat, you want to achieve the *highest* numbers on starboard tack and the *lowest* numbers on port. This explains why you may see 'starboard high — port low' written by the compass or along the boom of a competitor's boat.

Wind shadow

Wind shadow can affect the efficiency of your sails and is identified by a breakdown or reduced flow of air across the sails. Shadow can be caused by sailing too close to a cliff face, where the wind becomes disturbed, or by

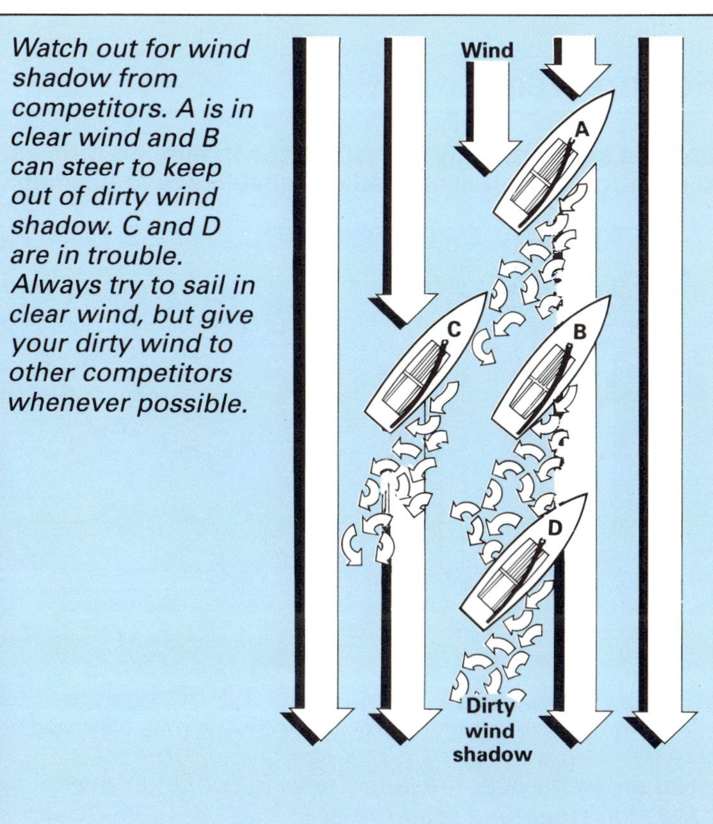

Watch out for wind shadow from competitors. A is in clear wind and B can steer to keep out of dirty wind shadow. C and D are in trouble. Always try to sail in clear wind, but give your dirty wind to other competitors whenever possible.

passing near to a ship or large yacht. When sailing in busy waters always plan your course to avoid wind shadow, which stretches farther than you think.

More serious when racing is the wind shadow created by competitors, and referred to as 'dirty wind'. All sailing boats create disturbed airflow, or turbulence from sails, and the closer you are to this turbulence, the more serious the effect. Your own wind shadow stretches back in the direction of the apparent wind as far as ten boatlengths.

When you sail into the wind shadow of your rivals, the first obvious effect is a reduction in the power of your sails and a falling off of boatspeed. If you were sitting out, then it might well be necessary to sit in to compensate. Naturally this effect can be used to great advantage against rivals, and with practice the exact point of overlap when the shadow takes effect can be identified.

Sea breezes

Breezes are created by a local change in temperature, and knowledge of their likelihood can enable you to position

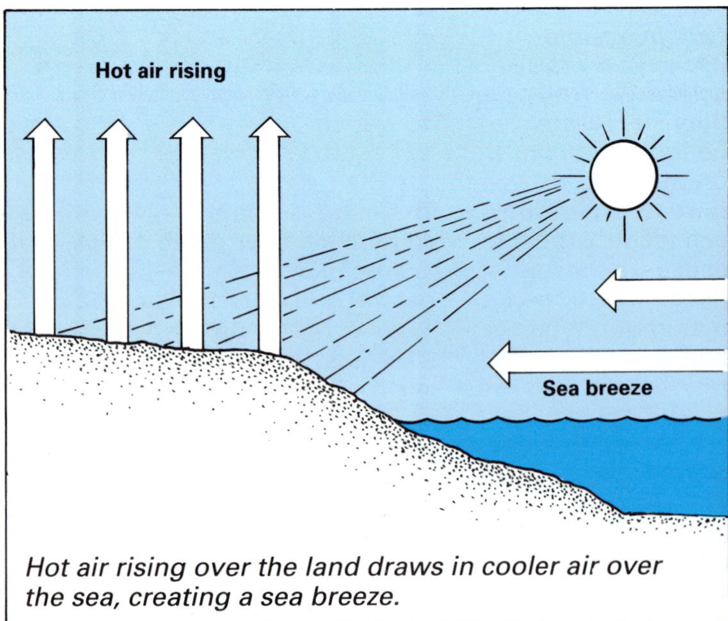

Hot air rising over the land draws in cooler air over the sea, creating a sea breeze.

yourself on the right side of the course to get the new wind.

Sea breezes are probably familiar to most sailors, and are caused by the sun warming the land mass, often many miles inland of the race course. Hot air thermals are created and the rapidly rising hot air is replaced by colder air drawn in from the sea. On a sunny day, with all the right conditions, a strong onshore breeze can be created, and this will occur at a regular time, usually around 1 p.m. As the sun begins to lose its warming power over the land the effect falls away and the breeze dies down, quite rapidly, usually around 4 p.m.

If conditions exist for the creation of a sea breeze (usually light onshore breezes in early morning with clear skies, and sunshine) then the crew should be on the lookout for a darker line on the horizon, denoting the rippled water surface as the gust of wind is sucked inshore (see also p.38).

Gusts on the water

Gusts of wind are at best an exciting increase in wind power, and at worst the cause of an unexpected capsize. It is important to watch out for clues as to when they might reach you, and you can practise this by sitting on the beach or lakeside and carefully watching gusts blowing across the water. Gusts tend not to be consistent, and they fan out to either side. Experienced sailors will always be looking ahead when sailing to windward, with one eye on the sailplan, one eye on the bow and waves, and the third (!) on the lookout for gusts. In calm conditions, you can identify the new wind by the darker patch of ripples it causes. In heavier winds, immediate response is necessary to keep the boat flat and boatspeed at the maximum. When sailing downwind, a gust will tickle the hair on the back of your neck just a second or so before it reaches the sails, enabling you to trim sails and balance accordingly.

Heavy gusts make sailing increasingly difficult, as trimming sails and balance become more important. Things can go wrong in a big way in these conditions, so as the gusts become more ferocious, increase the safety tolerance by sailing a safer, more manageable course. When beating to windward this may mean sailing just a

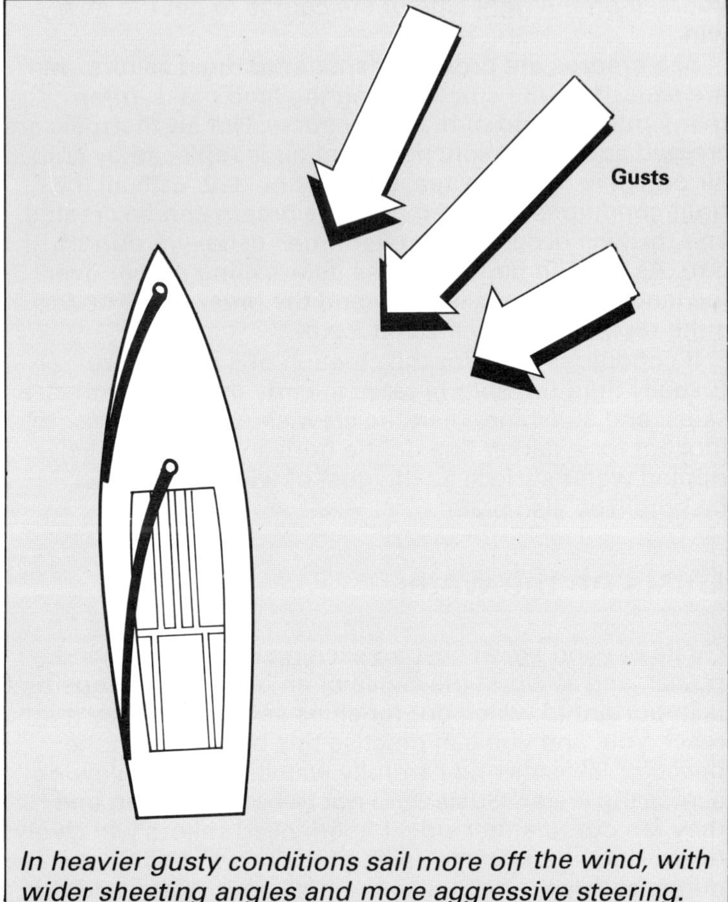

In heavier gusty conditions sail more off the wind, with wider sheeting angles and more aggressive steering.

little more off the wind than normal, but increased boatspeed will help compensate for the extra distance to be sailed, and the wider angle gives you more opportunity to steer through the gust.

●**Tip** Whether the wind is a gust or steady, you can easily gauge the direction of the wind by imagining a set square lying along the waves or ripples. With experience, you can sail your boat to windward, purely by judging the angle of the waves relative to the boat.

CHAPTER TEN

Sailing in light and medium winds

Lightwind sailing is all about maximum power and minimum drag; that means full sails, and no wash from the stern. To get rid of drag, the crew has to sit as far forward as possible, usually around the shrouds or farther forward, to keep the transom out of the water. Any movements should be slow and careful so as to minimize

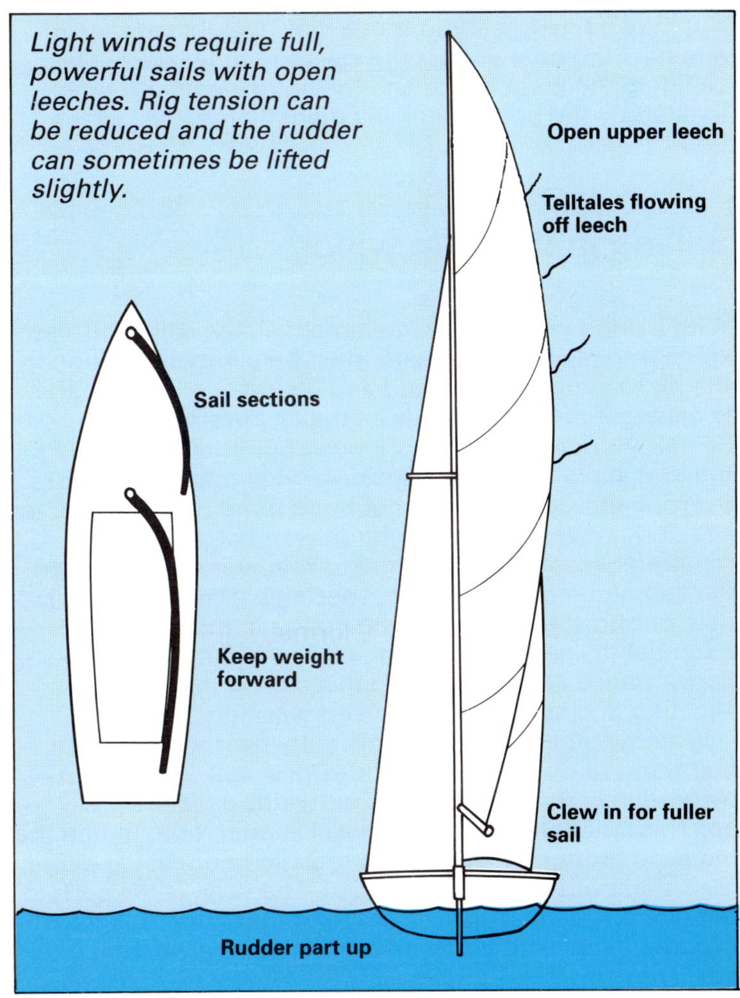

Light winds require full, powerful sails with open leeches. Rig tension can be reduced and the rudder can sometimes be lifted slightly.

rocking, and speed of action is forgone in favour of smoothness of control. Sails have to be trimmed at all times, and the winner is likely to be the one who has paid most attention to this.

Rig tension is not so important because the mast is not going to bend much. If the wind is very light then reduce the tension, and allow the sails to sag just a little. Also, expect little forestay sag to fill the luff of the sail. This is a time when tell-tales (p.21) are invaluable, and although sails should be set as full as conditions will allow, the leech of both mainsail and genoa (or jib) should be open, to reduce stall of airflow across the sails.

It may be necessary to move crew weight to leeward and heel the boat so that the sails sag to leeward. This will help them set better and the extra weather helm created by the boat's heel will magnify the 'feel' of the boat.

Sailing in medium winds

With a good working breeze almost all the sail controls come into play. Firstly, there must be plenty of tension in the rig to control mast bend and jib luff sag. After that, it is necessary to set the sails as full as possible without being overpowered. This is when your stomach and leg muscles have to be used because what may be overpowering to you may not be to more experienced, (or heavier) crews. If your weight does not provide the required ballast, you will need to keep very fit, and learn the technique of sitting out/trapezing without too much pain or effort, to maximize the power in the rig. It is essential to keep the boat flat, or nearly flat, for best performance at all times, and this means that sail sheeting and steering become increasingly important.

When you begin to be consistently overpowered, the first thing to do is to flatten the largest sail — the main — by gradually moving the clew outwards as far as it will go. This will flatten the overall sail shape. Next, flatten the mainsail further by forcing the mast to bend, using either mainsheet or vang (kicking strap). The vang is the current popular choice in most classes, and these controls have become increasingly powerful, often with a working efficiency of 16 to 1 or even 24 to 1 for just this purpose.

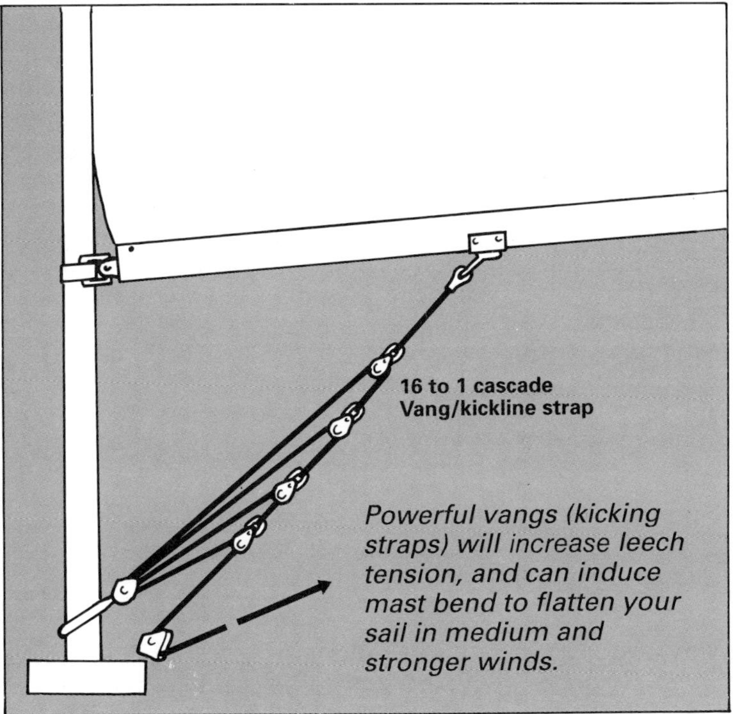

When the mast bends, the mainsail will (or should) flatten, dramatically reducing power, and making it easier for your, by now, tired muscles to keep the boat flat. With increased winds and boatspeed, the crew should concentrate their weight farther aft towards the centre, athwartships, position. Each differing dinghy design will have an established position. Now the bow needs to be able to lift, but without the stern dragging, so move around until you get the balance right.

Off the wind, watch out for the chance that the boat will plane, rapidly accelerating forward, because then crew weight should move aft quickly to keep the boat up and planing. Remember, however, to move back to the original position if the boat slows. For medium winds it is still necessary to sit forward when sailing downwind, and again by shuffling up and down the side deck you will find a position that feels right for the boat. Often, the crew will sit to leeward, enabling the helm to sit on the opposite side to balance, see forward and keep an eye on the sailplan and the waves.

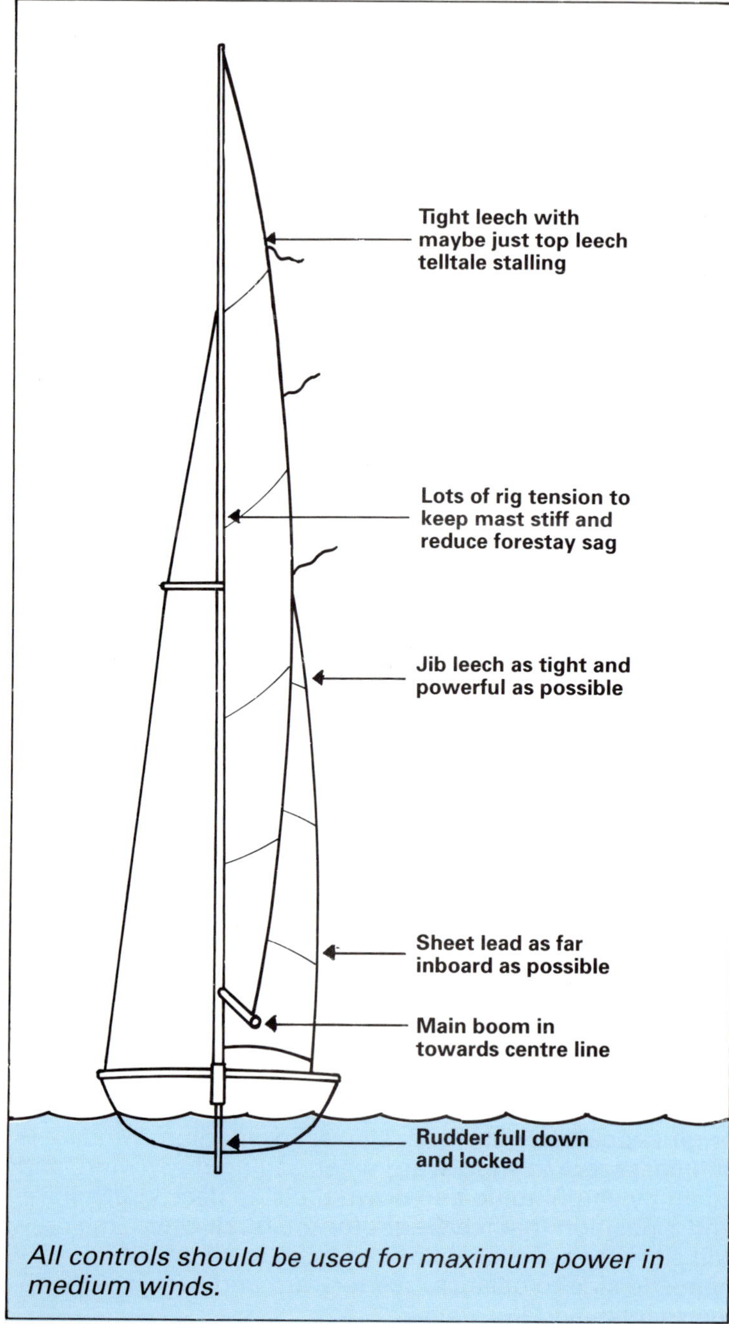

All controls should be used for maximum power in medium winds.

CHAPTER ELEVEN

Surviving a blow

Sailing in strong winds is both exciting and nerve-racking — will you survive, make a fool of yourself, wreck the boat, or even win? It is important to differentiate between sailing in strong winds for speed — when you are still going for gold and in control — and sailing for survival, when you are trying to get home without too much damage to either yourself or the boat.

Sailing for speed

There are two areas to concentrate on here: keeping the flattest possible sailplan for best control; and keeping the

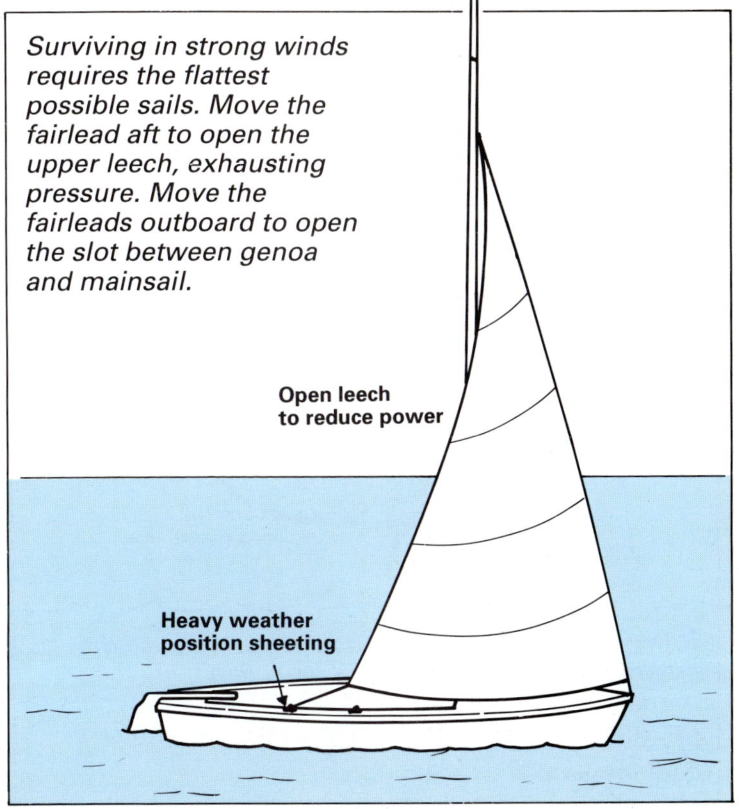

Surviving in strong winds requires the flattest possible sails. Move the fairlead aft to open the upper leech, exhausting pressure. Move the fairleads outboard to open the slot between genoa and mainsail.

boat itself as flat as possible as all times. Much of the sail flattening process can be done on the shore, and this should include any increase to the rake of the mast. The clew position should be locked out at the maximum, and in order to open the leech of the jib, the sheet lead should be moved aft and, possibly, outboard.

The rudder needs to be locked in the fully down position, and the vang loaded 'until your eyes bulge', as the saying goes — the description is apt for many classes. With the vang tight, a good amount of bend in the mast giving a flat mainsail, and an open leeched jib, you are ready for action. If the boat is still overpowered when sailing to windward, then you could reduce power even more by lifting some of the centreboard, but obviously you will not climb to windward so well. Now, the challenge is to sail flat, fast and manageably, against being overpowered, heeling and pointing high. Try it!

If you feel confident enough to give the spinnaker an airing, then plan the setting carefully. Before launching the kite, reduce the centreboard even farther to allow the boat to slip sideways in the gusts. It is also wise to reduce

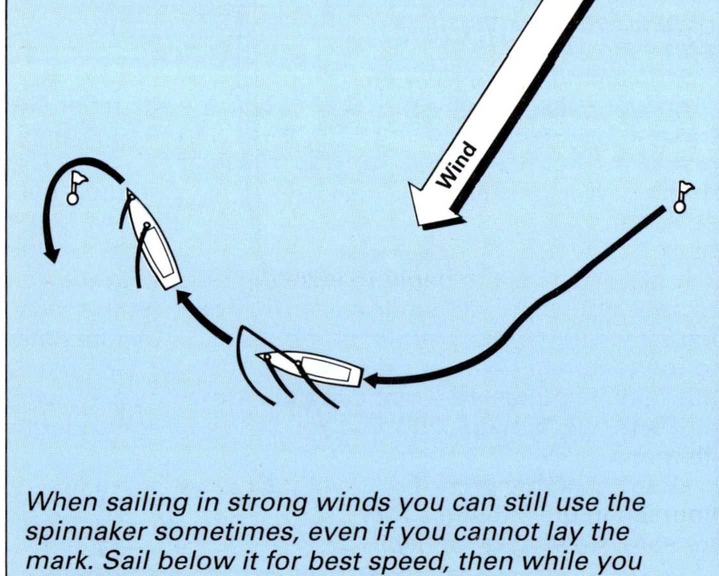

When sailing in strong winds you can still use the spinnaker sometimes, even if you cannot lay the mark. Sail below it for best speed, then while you can still close reach to the mark, take the spinnaker down.

vang tension, so that the mainsail leech is softer. Try to sail as fast as possible, reducing the pressure in the about-to-be-filled sail. Once up and set, the spinnaker should make the boat more stable, and a lot faster. Things usually go wrong at the launch, gybe, or recovery, so concentrate on planning the manoeuvres and executing them quickly and decisively. For good spinnaker work, the pole height and guy need to be set carefully, with the pole usually set higher for stronger winds.

When a strong gust hits, remember to bear away hard, and ease the sheets. This will keep the boat steady, and increase speed at the same time. If you are blown down below your course,do not panic, but think about how long you can hold on to the spinnaker without missing the mark. It is often possible to sail three-quarters of a reaching leg with the spinnaker, then drop and beam or close reach up to fetch the mark.

If you are about to gybe, think twice: there are times when a tack will be much safer, and keep you in the race. In these conditions it is often the survivors who get good positions, or even win!

Sailing for survival

Any honest sailor will admit that at some stage he or she has run for cover and decided to abandon the race, happy just to get home in one piece. It is important to make the decision to quit quite clearly in your mind, and then sail a safe, conservative course while you plan how best to get back to shore.

It is a good idea to begin to ease the tension in the vang to save your sails and equipment. Try not to let the sails flap, because this is when the most damage can be done to the material. Dropping the mainsail can be considered, but only if you are sure you can get it down quickly, safely and without damage, and that you can get back under the jib alone.

When sailing downwind to homebase try not to involve yourself in questionable manoeuvres like gybing, and go for safe, slow tacks followed by bearing away in a series of broad reaches. Remember to ease the sails through all the gusts. It will often pay to keep the sheets out of any cleats or jamming devices until you are more sure that the gusts can be managed. Good luck!

CHAPTER TWELVE

Steering

Just as it is impossible to control a car with slack in the steering and the front wheel nuts loose, you will not get the best from your boat if the rudder unit is slack, bendy or worn.

Rudders and tillers

The tiller needs to be strong, and tightly secured to the blade so that there is no twist in the unit, because there will be times when you really need to be forceful with it, such as during a gybe, or to avoid a collision. The tiller extension, although just a piece of tubing, is very important to you because it is the helmsman's real contact with the machine — the joystick if you like! Spend a little time getting it to feel right in the hand, and make sure that it is coated, because in cold weather, cold aluminium tubing can soon make your fingers numb. On unloved boats there is often a loose and ragged universal joint between tiller and extension, with lots of slack, and this is another area where a little expenditure can bring about a worthwhile improvement.

One of the most important factors that affect steering is the 'down' position of the rudder blade. In light winds you can get much more feel through the rudder by having the blade partially up (if class rules allow), but in any strength of wind it is essential to get the rudder blade right down and lock it there. When leaving the shore there is often a slight movement of the blade backwards, so it is always worth checking this as soon as you get settled.

One of the great hidden tricks of fast sailing is the fine tuning of the rudder 'down' position. If you get standard gear with your dinghy, check the class rules carefully and see what facility there is for adjustment, because on many

•**Tip** Good drill for all sailors is to practise manoeuvres without using the rudder. This soon teaches you the effect of heel and trim on steering.

dinghies getting the rudder really vertical, and locked tightly in place, will improve the balance on the helm, and enable you to drive with more control and 'feel'.

Weather and lee helm

In order to understand how well a boat is balanced, it is necessary to have some knowledge about the forces that can help steer a sailing craft. From the overall sailplan the Centre of Effort (C of E) can be determined, i.e. the 'balance' point of the force generated by the aerofoils. Likewise, the Centre of Lateral Resistance (CLR), the 'balance' point representing the resistance force to sideways motion, can be determined, somewhere around the centreboard area. These two forces working against each other determine if the dinghy will sail up into the wind, or sail away from the wind if you let go of the tiller.

When the C of E is behind the CLR, then the boat will want to sail into the wind; this is 'weather helm'. With the CLR behind the C of E, then the dinghy will want to bear away; this is 'lee helm'. Sailing dinghies should be set up with a little weather helm, to give a touch of weight or 'feel' to the steering. The rudder is, of course, contributing to the CLR. With a well balanced boat the weather helm effect will be increased by heeling to leeward, and reduced by heeling to windward. When sailing dinghies are badly out of balance, the head of the mast can usually be moved, or raked, to compensate. Rake also affects weather helm, as it moves the sailplan aft and the C of E with it.

CHAPTER THIRTEEN

Directions and manoeuvres

There are several manoeuvres that are common to all sailing craft, whether they be yachts, windsurfers or dinghies, and although the basics are straightforward, getting the best out of the manoeuvre can be more difficult. For best performance, the first thing to remember is that the fewest number of manoeuvres will save most time and slow the boat down as little as possible. When you decide to make a manoeuvre, always

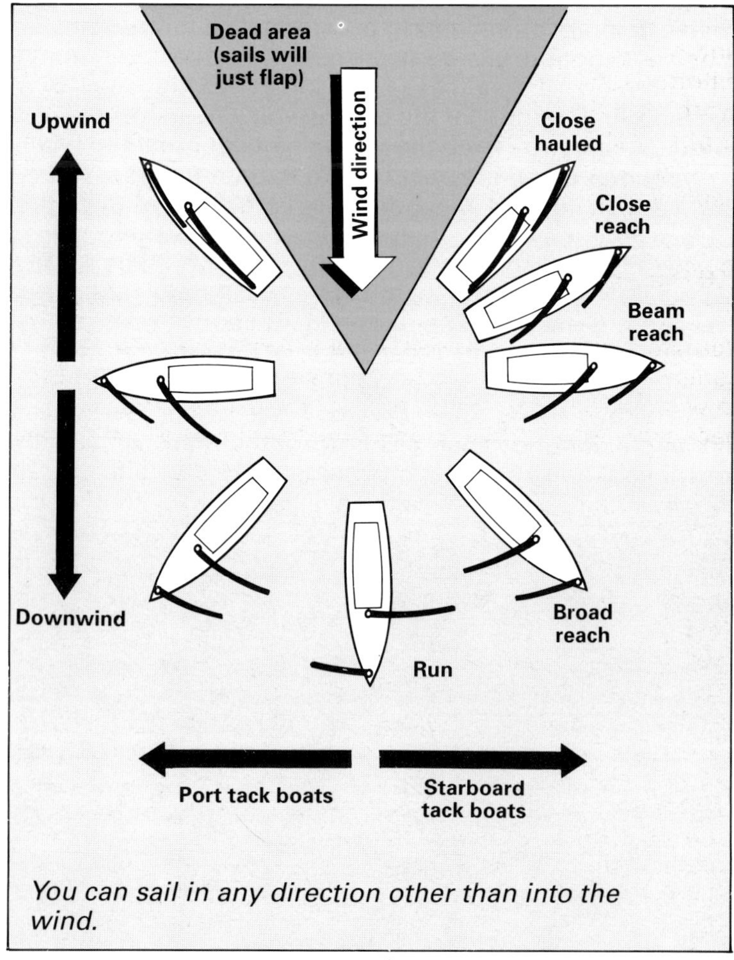

You can sail in any direction other than into the wind.

try to plan it carefully so that you come away from it as fast as possible and in the right direction.

The direction in which you travel is determined by the interaction of the steering at the hull with the setting of sails above it. When you get it wrong you can end up swimming! There are many combinations of direction and sail trim, and there are several basic descriptions and manoeuvres.

Close-hauled

You are close-hauled, or beating, to windward when your sails are trimmed as close as possible to the centreline, and you are pointing as near as possible to the wind without your sails stalling or lifting. If they do, you are too close, and the front of your sails (luff) will back wind. This is often called luffing, or pinching. Sailing to windward on a close-hauled course is critical for speed tuning, as it usually occurs in the first leg of the race.

Reaching

You are reaching when your sails are set free, off the centreline, and your direction does not require you to tack to windward to get to the mark. This term is fairly vague, because you can be reaching from the moment you just

•**Tip** Everyone knows that a straight line is the shortest distance between two points, but when sailing it is often not the fastest. When you are beating for instance, because the wind is steady in neither direction, nor strength, there will be times when it will pay to 'pinch', and other times when the best option is to sail free. A stronger gust may enable you to sail higher for best boatspeed and VMG (see p.52) and a patch of lighter wind will require the sails to be eased, for more power and faster speed. If the course was plotted, it would form a wavy line to windward, and it is likely that experienced sailors would sail a more erratic line than beginners, to take best advantage of speed and direction.

> •**Tip** When running, sailing the shortest distance makes sense, but the boat will go all the faster when turned slightly on to a broad reach. Over 1-2 miles (2-3 km) the difference in speed can be dramatic, so by reaching a little, rather than running square, the boatspeed advantage will probably more than compensate for the longer distance to be sailed.

ease your sheets from a beat (close reaching) right around to when you are broad reaching, almost a run.

Running

You are running when the wind comes from behind the dinghy, and your sails are eased out as far as safety will allow. Here, the wind effectively pushes the boat along, which is the way the old square-rigged ships used the wind in most cases.

The VMG factor

This is a new term that has filtered down from ocean racing and is now heard around sailing club bars. It stands for Velocity Made Good and relates to the difference between pointing the boat as closely as

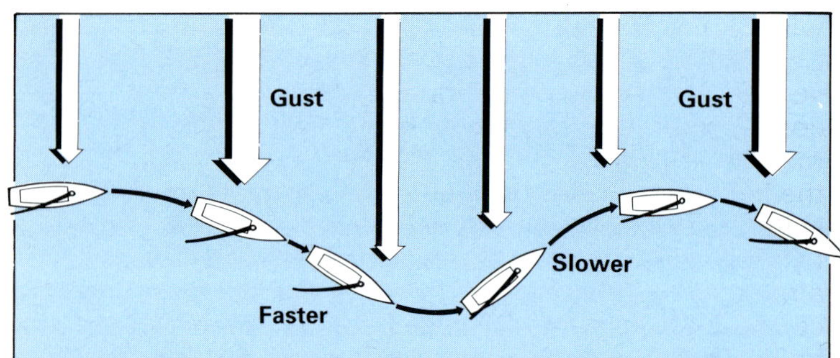

When reaching it will pay to bear away when a gust hits. The boat will accelerate, and as the wind gets lighter, steer higher to get back on course.

•Tip Reaching tends to be a steadier course, but when gusts hit, boatspeed can be increased dramatically by easing sails slightly and sailing off the wind until the gust has passed. With lighter wind you then recover your direction by climbing a little higher, so even when reaching, the fastest course to the reaching mark is an erratic zigzag — not a straight line.

possible towards the mark when beating or running with a loss of speed, and sailing a faster, wider course. The term derives from the computer system that works out whether it is going to be faster to point high, or sail fuller. In a dinghy you have to sail by the seat of your pants, and make these judgments yourself. It is interesting to observe the difference in pointing between different fast sailors in any fleet. Often at the start, the fleet will quickly fan out, with some boats sailing high, and others almost reaching, sailing farther but faster. At the windward mark the fleet will close up again. It is important to decide whether you are going to 'pinch' or 'sail free', and this is something that should be experimented with regularly.

Tacking

Tacking is when the front of the boat passes through the wind direction and the boom crosses the centreline of the boat. Before tacking, get the sheets prepared and make sure that there will be no foul-ups. It is a good idea to come off the wind slightly to increase speed for the manoeuvre, and to choose the right area of flat water. Sail the boat around, keeping all the sheets hard in until the sails back wind, then ease the mainsheet and let the jib fly. Recovering, it is important to get the sails sheeted almost all the way in quickly and get on to the new course, but momentarily to sail free, to pick up speed, before gently squeezing the sheets for final trimming.

When practising, count in seconds as you go through the manoeuvre, and you will see that it is rhythm, and not just speed, that makes a good tack. Helm and crew should work together, bringing the sails in, and easing, in unison.

Gybing

Gybing is the more complicated manoeuvre, in which the mainsail crosses from one side of the boat to the other when sailing downwind. When gybing, the pressures on both hull and sailplan change dramatically, so this is a time for positive and decisive action. Again careful planning is necessary, because although experts make it look simple, they choose the exact piece of water or wave on which to execute the manoeuvre, and gybe with the least amount of pressure in the sails. This may mean that they would sail 50 or 100 yards (metres) after deciding to gybe, just to get the conditions right.

The stronger the wind, the more wind pressure in the rig, which means the greater the potential problems, so you should gybe when you are sailing at maximum speed, usually when surfing down a wave.

Often the mainsail can be flipped across the centreline very easily when going fast and the pressure is transposed from side to side without a problem. If the wind strength allows, grab the whole sheet system and pull it across, especially if you have a lot of purchases, rather than haul in lots of rope.

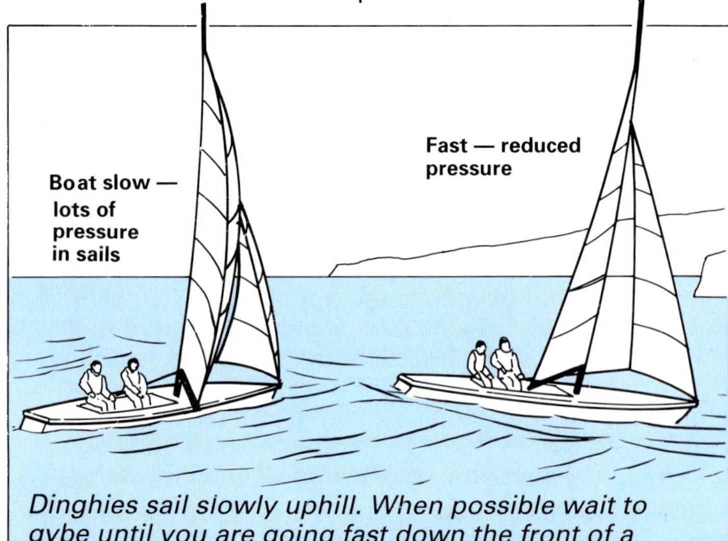

Dinghies sail slowly uphill. When possible wait to gybe until you are going fast down the front of a wave, and this will reduce apparent wind pressure in the sails.

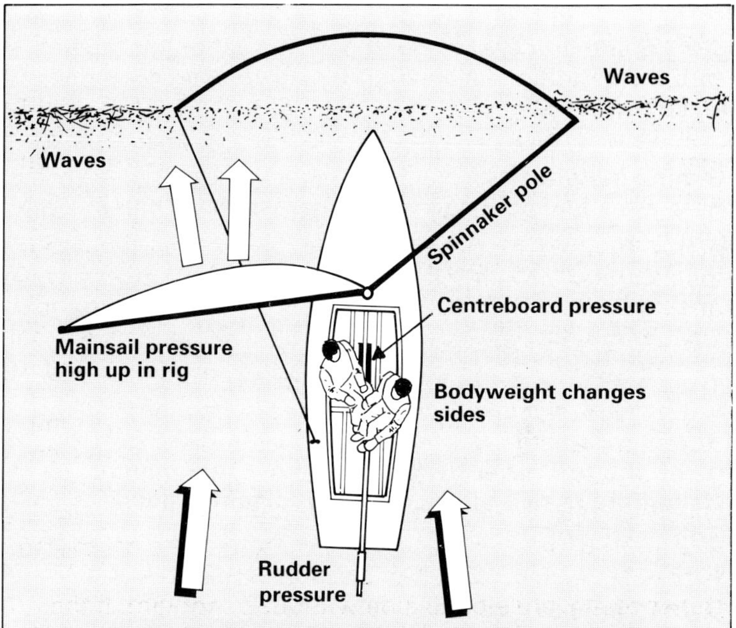

Waves

Waves

Spinnaker pole

Centreboard pressure

Mainsail pressure high up in rig

Bodyweight changes sides

Rudder pressure

Pressure in the sails will change as the boat gybes. This has to be balanced by crew weight and good steering. On the gybe the helmsman and crew both cross to their new positions. With helm and crew near the centre line the boat will be "tender" downwind. When they sit outboard the boat becomes less "tippy".

A decisive heave on the mainsheet will get you through the gybe quickly.

There are different techniques for light and strong wind gybing, but you always need decisive action on the helm, with the conditions as favourable as you can possibly make them.

Gybing in light airs
Here are a few points to remember when gybing in light airs.

- **Very little centre board needed**
- **Flip main across with hand**
- **Move very carefully to stop rocking boat**
- **Minimum of rudder movement**
- **Stay well forward to keep transom out**
- **After gybe, sail up slightly to increase flow and therefore speed**
- **Keep the spinnaker flying throughout manoeuvre**
- **Take time to reset pole; more importantly, keep spinnaker flying**

Gybing in heavy winds
Here are some tips for gybing in heavy winds.

- **Look for flatter water**
- **Gybe when going downhill fast**
- **Prepare crew for fast reaction to any roll**
- **Get some mainsheet in before sailing into gybe**
- **Be decisive with tiller, sail into gybe (helm up)**
- **Immediately boom crosses, get the boat's heading back by reverse action (helm up on new tack)**
- **Keep kicker on firmly to stop leech twist in main, which would roll boat in**

Of all manoeuvres, the gybe is the one that is really worth practising, because it will give you increased confidence when you get out racing. Try to string together gybe after gybe, in quick succession, and you will soon begin to sort out a rhythm for the manoeuvre.

Rounding marks

It is possible to improve dramatically your position during a race by good mark rounding. Again, planning the manoeuvre well ahead makes all the difference. Your

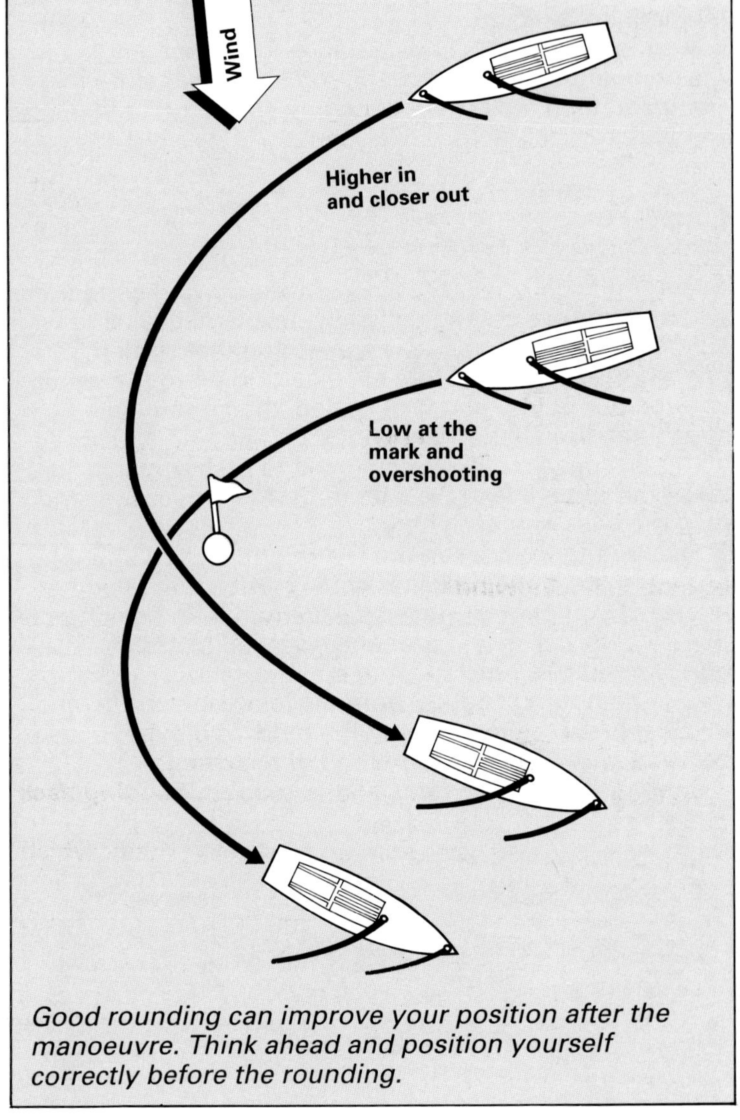

Good rounding can improve your position after the manoeuvre. Think ahead and position yourself correctly before the rounding.

decision on how and where to position yourself will be affected by other boats around you. How close you are as you approach the mark is not important, rather your proximity as you *leave* it.

If you turn too tightly, then the boat will be slowed by pressure on rudder, centreboard and sails, but if you sail a wider, more gentle curve, the boat's movement will be maintained for longer.

Racing rules give a considerable advantage to the inside boat position at a mark, so plan ahead to be that boat, and then make your rounding correctly for you, and to the detriment of your opponent.

Capsizing

Capsizing usually takes place in stronger wind conditions when things are getting distinctly problematical, and what action to take in a capsize is something that should be given consideration before even getting on to the water. If your boat is sound and well sealed, then immediately after a capsize all the activity of sails flapping and spray flying disappears. There is no need to rush or panic, just take your time, even take a short break if necessary and plan the best way of righting.

Recovering from a capsize is straightforward enough, but there are some tricks to employ when things go wrong. If you get the mast stuck in mud then heaving on the windward side will probably succeed in getting the boat up with the mast broken, and the sails torn. Get a rescue boat to pull gently from the leeward shroud, and this will draw the mast out of the mud, and then you can proceed with the normal method of recovery.

If the boat is full of water, fill the sails cautiously at first,

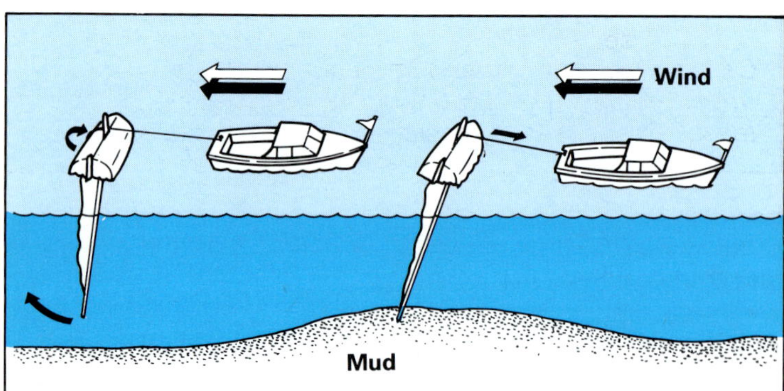

For normal righting with assistance, tie the rope over the boat and to the chainplate. This will turn the boat as the tow starts.

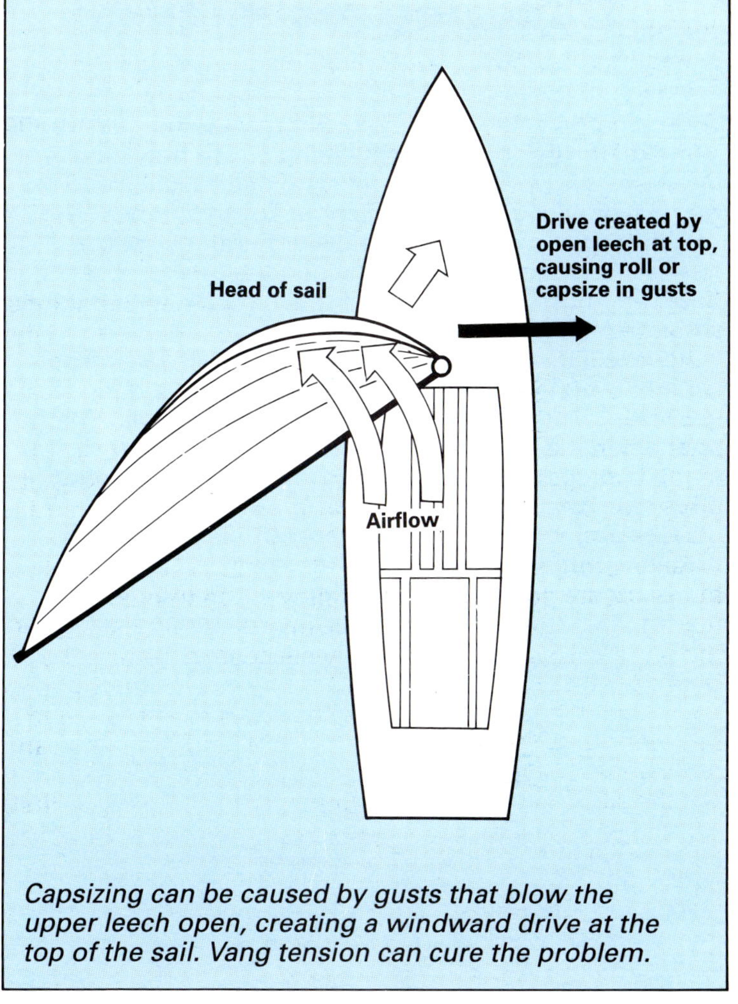

Capsizing can be caused by gusts that blow the upper leech open, creating a windward drive at the top of the sail. Vang tension can cure the problem.

because you will have dramatically increased the weight of the boat, and this will strain the rig and possibly stretch and damage your sails.

After capsize try and find the reason for it by talking to other sailors who can identify the problem because they have already experienced it themselves. There can be a number of reasons for your mishap; it could be simply not enough vang (kicking strap) tension, which allows the sail to twist too much at the top, driving the top mast to windward, and creating the upset.

CHAPTER FOURTEEN

Trapezing techniques

Turbo-charge your dinghy with a trapeze! That just about sums up the performance advantage from trapezing — it increases the power-to-weight ratio dramatically and has many more advantages, and some disadvantages. The 'trapeze artist' can also move his or her body weight forward or aft just by walking along the gunwale, and it is possible to concentrate weight much better, with the helm sitting alongside the crew's legs.

Always launch yourself from the side with your front leg and keep this one straight, bending the back leg as necessary. This will stop you rolling down the side of the boat when it decelerates. The jib sheet will also lock you to the side of the boat and reduce the constant forward drive from the angle of the trapeze wire.

Trapezing when sailing to windward presents no real problem, but when reaching, the crew need to move well aft along the gunwale, increasing the forward pull from the trapeze wire. If the boat hits a wave and is slowed, or

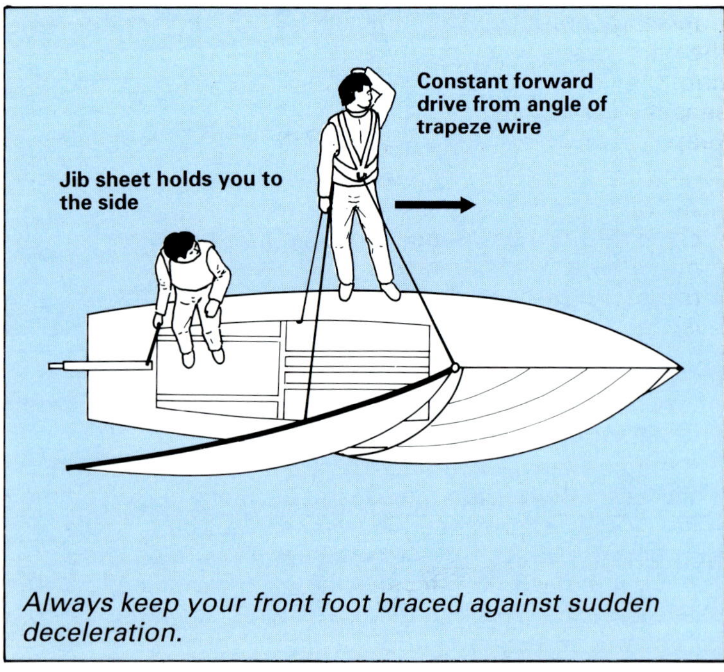

Always keep your front foot braced against sudden deceleration.

more seriously power-dives into a wave and stops, then the trapezing crew can take off in a roller-coaster ride along the gunwale, towards the bow. It has even been known for the crew to go round the bow and up on the other side, which can be nasty! That is why you should keep your legs about 2 feet (60cm) apart when trapezing, until you are experienced enough to handle the 'roller-coaster'. Sometimes, a toe-loop in a convenient place can help.

Getting across the boat from tack to tack needs practice, but once you are confident, you can actually launch yourself over the side just holding the trapeze handle and jib sheet. A quick pull on the sheet into its cleat gets the jib sorted out, then the free hand picks up the trapeze ring and connects it to the hook — this system is really fast, but it needs practice and a fearless crew!

For good trapezing, it will probably be necessary to improve the non-slip finish along the gunwale, and to get a really good pair of sailing shoes. This will give a lot of extra grip, particularly on wild, wet windy days when you need it.

The amount of crew power can be increased or reduced by changing the height of the trapeze ring. In marginal trapezing conditions the ring needs to be higher, and as the wind pressure increases, you should lower the ring until the crew is actually level with the gunwale. In bumpy seas the crew may need to trapeze higher — partly to keep dry, and also reduce drag if you hit a big wave!

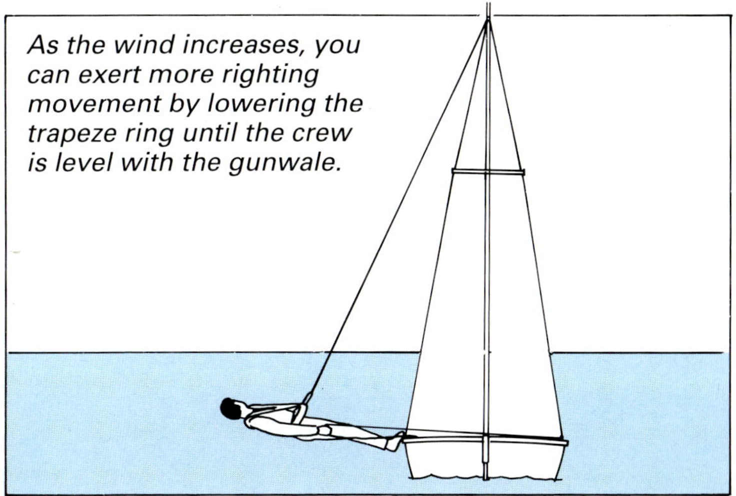

As the wind increases, you can exert more righting movement by lowering the trapeze ring until the crew is level with the gunwale.

Interestingly, there is very much less windspeed skimming along the top of the waves at sea level, than at even 5 feet (1.5m) higher, so there is an additional advantage in staying at low as possible.

When sailing single-handed, the same theory of trapezing applies, but make sure that you check the adjustment rope regularly. Although it can be a problem in a two-man dinghy when the crew suddenly disappears in the briny, it is more of a disaster when you are single-handed!

There is a whole range of trapeze belts on the market, from the hi-tech variety featuring leg straps with buckles to simple rope-tie belts. Preference is a matter for each individual sailor, but the belt should be reasonably comfortable for long periods on the trapeze, and reasonably secure, so that it does not come undone while sailing.

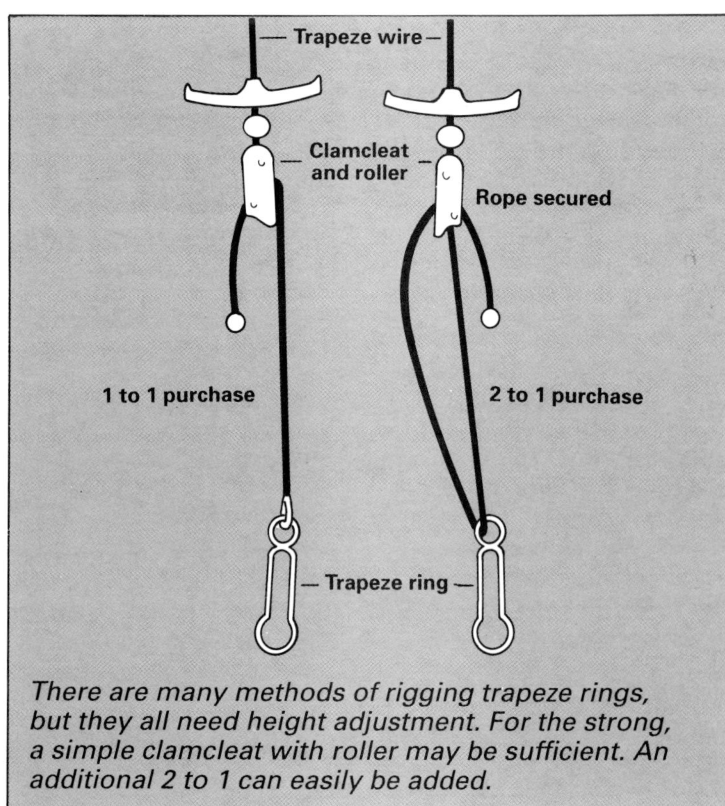

There are many methods of rigging trapeze rings, but they all need height adjustment. For the strong, a simple clamcleat with roller may be sufficient. An additional 2 to 1 can easily be added.

CHAPTER FIFTEEN

Racing: are you ready to mix?

There is nothing better than the waterborne three-dimensional chess game of dinghy racing, but how do you get started? Most clubs run races, and for the more serious, each class holds open regattas at different venues around the country, culminating in National, European and World Championships.

Do not expect to do well on your first race, but just get into the starting area, keeping well clear of other more experienced boats, and plan to get around the course. A good idea is to start behind the others on your first outing, and by observing them you will soon get a feel of when to tack, and how much distance to leave at marks. As you begin to gain more practical experience you will identify the need to know more about the rules and tactics (see p.65). The Racing Rules, established and updated regularly by the IYRU, are 'for the organization, conduct and judging of the sport of yacht racing', and primarily invoked to avoid collisions on the course. You will not learn them all at once, but the essential rules can be picked up quite quickly. So you will need a copy of the rule book to refer to (available from any chandlery shop). Many sailors use a book called *Paul Elvstrom Explains the Yacht Racing Rules*, mainly because of the little model boats included with it!

Tactics are another discipline, but with a good knowledge of the rules, you can position yourself to your advantage, and often to the disadvantage of your competitors. The subject of tactics and their application, from the simplest luffing before the race start, to complex covering and blocking manoeuvres, could fill a large book.

Under tow

If you race regularly, there will be occasions when you have to get towed home, and sometimes towed out to the start. Always have a long, strong rope available, or be ready to disconnect the jib sheet.

The most solid place to attach a tow is to the mast, and preferably as low down as possible, and if there is more

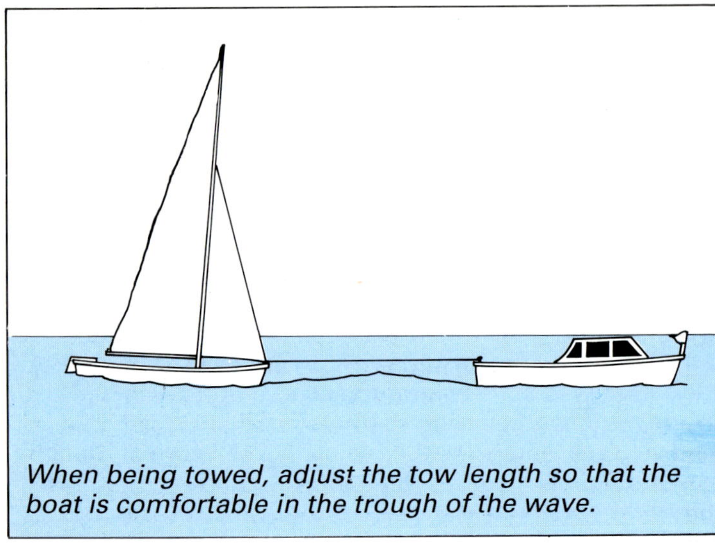
When being towed, adjust the tow length so that the boat is comfortable in the trough of the wave.

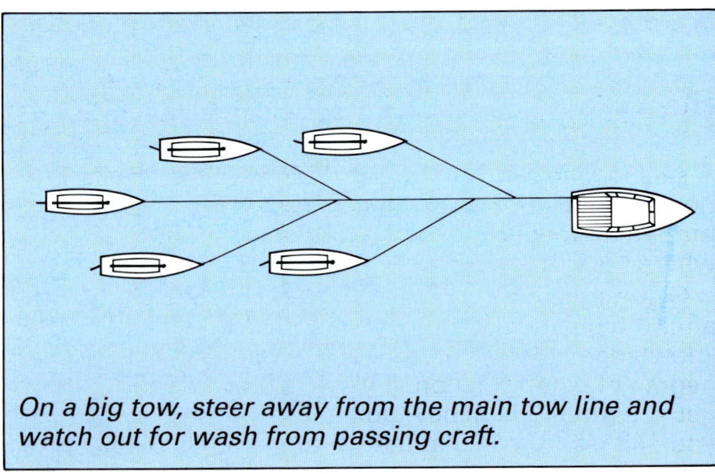
On a big tow, steer away from the main tow line and watch out for wash from passing craft.

than one crew, it is best to just take a few turns, and then hold. This will enable you to slip the rope if anything goes wrong. Allow the boat to slide sideways by reducing the centreboard, and adjust the length of towline so that the boat sits comfortably in the trough of any wash created by the towing craft.

At regattas with large numbers of competitors the tow craft may just drag a long line, and you will have to sail over, tie on with a rolling hitch, or other secure knot, and steer slightly off the line for safety.

CHAPTER SIXTEEN

Racing rules and tactics

Although racing rules are mentioned here, their application needs careful analysis. It is strongly recommended that you should have a set of rules before you start mixing with other boats, and that you should be particularly aware of the rules for prevention of collision. The IYRU rules also define exactly the point when you complete a manoeuvre, and therefore when you do and do not have rights over other boats.

This book assumes that you already have some basic knowledge of the fundamental rules of port tack yachts giving way to starboard yachts (on opposite tacks), and windward yachts keeping clear of leeward yachts (on the same tack). These rules and others are often quoted, but there are circumstances when they can be overridden, and so the safe resolution is always to have the rule book to hand when racing.

Starting

A sailing club can set any course it likes, but wherever possible it is normal to start with a windward leg. Always make sure that you write the course down somewhere where you can refer to it.

Getting the dinghy to cross the line one second or less after the gun, and at full speed, requires a good working knowledge of the rules, lots of practice, and a certain degree of determination. If you are going to try hard to get it 'spot-on' then inevitably sometimes you will find yourself over the line at the start, as every experienced sailor has done in the past. With a fast return to clear the line and concentrating on sailing in clear air, there is no reason why you should not still do well – indeed on many occasions, circumstances like this bring out the best in more experienced yachtsmen.

The starting line and bias

A starting line is very seldom square to the wind, and knowing which end is farther to windward can give you a big advantage at the start. Remember that the more rivals you get behind you at the start, the clearer wind you will have, and the more quickly you will be able to reach the all-important first windward mark.

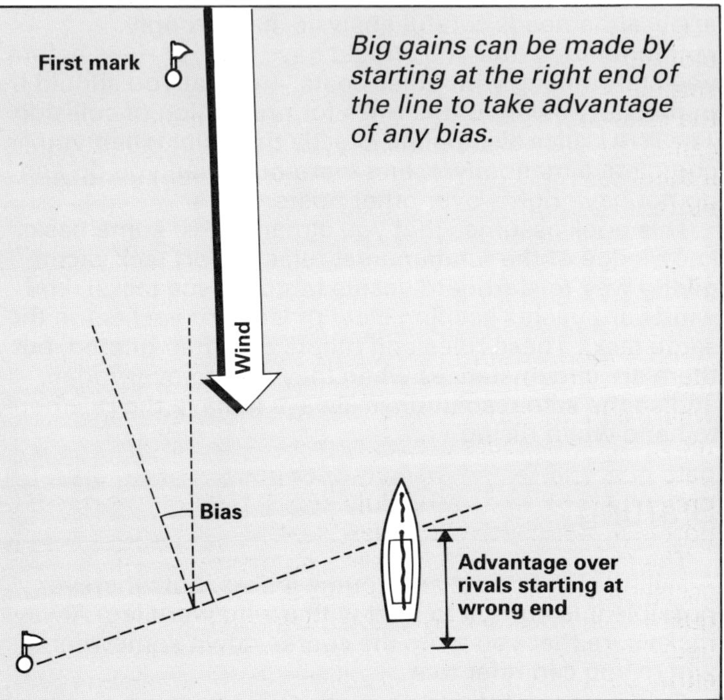

First mark

Wind

Bias

Advantage over rivals starting at wrong end

Big gains can be made by starting at the right end of the line to take advantage of any bias.

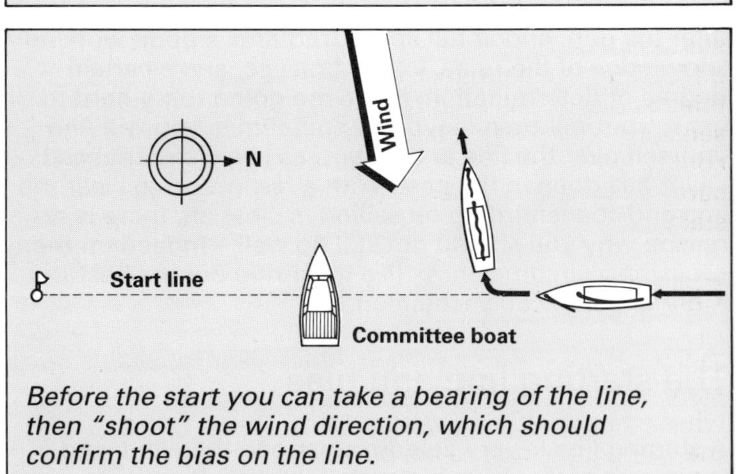

Before the start you can take a bearing of the line, then "shoot" the wind direction, which should confirm the bias on the line.

To find the amount of bias, take a compass bearing along the line, and then 'shoot' the boat directly into the wind, again taking a bearing. The difference between the wind bearing and the line bearing plus 90 degrees is the bias, and should decide your starting end.

It is possible to get a general idea of bias if you reach along the line in one direction, then without changing the settings on your sheets, tack the boat around and see if the sails set the same on the other tack. However, it cannot be claimed that this system is accurate, especially if there are many other boats on the line, and there is current running.

Gate starts

A more modern starting system, and arguably fairer, is the gate start. This system is often used with big fleets, where a long (and possibly biased) line would be required, and would probably prove uncontrollable. A gate boat is selected (usually 10th position from the previous race) and at the duly appointed time starts off on port tack, complete with guardboat.

The fleet position themselves so that they can accelerate on starboard, passing the leeward side of the guard boat. After a reasonable distance on port tack, usually 2 to 3 minutes, the gate boat is released, and can either continue on port tack, or go about on to starboard.

This system usually makes for a really even line at the start, and because everyone starts on starboard, it is difficult to be able to tack on to port for some time. If you think you can sail faster than the gate boat, then it is sensible to start early, because after 2 or 3 minutes, you could have some distance over rivals starting last. Tide or current may also influence your decision on where to start.

First leg

The most important time for sailing fast is just after the start, and up to the first windward mark, because that is where the greatest concentration of boats, and therefore the best position, is to be found. If there is a windshift advantage on the other tack, then use it if you can and go

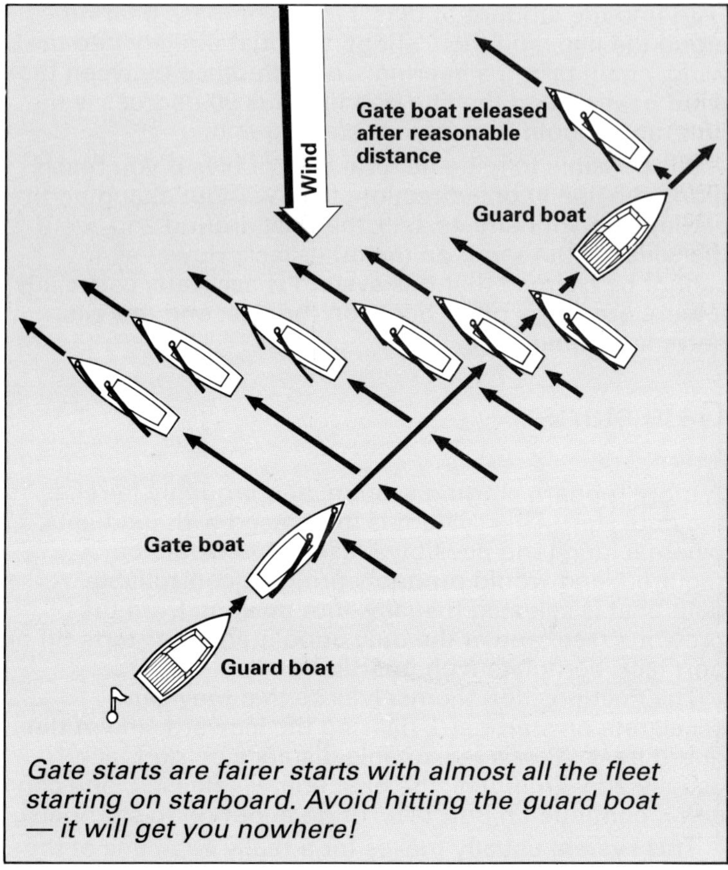

Gate starts are fairer starts with almost all the fleet starting on starboard. Avoid hitting the guard boat — it will get you nowhere!

about. Try always to sail in clear air, because at a time when most of the fleet are sailing away, wind shadow can slow you down considerably. If you are boxed in, and cannot tack, then it is worth considering sailing free and fast to clear your wind. You may lose distance to windward in the short term, but gaining speed and clear air is in the long run by far the best option.

Try to keep an eye on the leaders, because if they are sharp, and tack on the shifts, then it will give you a warning of a shift ahead. On a course with more than one class of boat, watching other fleets can be invaluable for clues to wind direction and other changes. Try not to get involved in racing against other individual boats, because this will cost you valuable concentration from your main task — to beat *every* boat in the fleet, not just one.

Crossing on port and starboard

How you choose to approach the windward mark does depend on how close you are to the front of the fleet, because of the increasing blanketing effect as more and more boats round the mark. The safe approach to the mark is always on starboard, but that is also the popular approach.

Although you may have starboard rights over an opponent, it sometimes pays to waive those rights and let

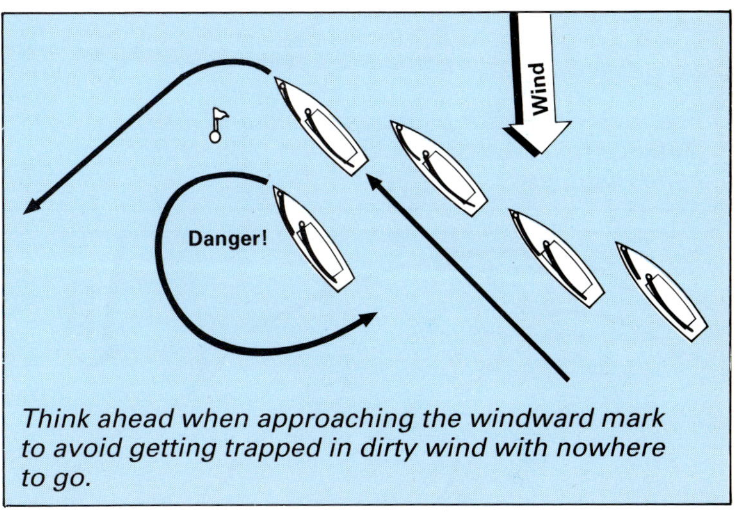

Think ahead when approaching the windward mark to avoid getting trapped in dirty wind with nowhere to go.

the port-hand boat across. Decide where you want to go, and in which direction you want your opponent to go, and then make your decision to wave him across, or call your rights. Remember that he can tack under you and create the lee-bow effect (p.71), forcing you to tack away! When giving way to a starboard-hand boat, you can lose the least distance by easing sheets and bearing away gently, carefully watching the other boat's transom. This will give you more speed to compensate for the loss of ground to windward.

When you are lucky enough to be in the first few rounding a mark, take advantage of every shift right up to the mark, to get up as much speed as possible for the rounding itself. Even ducking a boat at the mark will probably cost you nothing. If it looks as though a few boats are making their approach on starboard, then a port

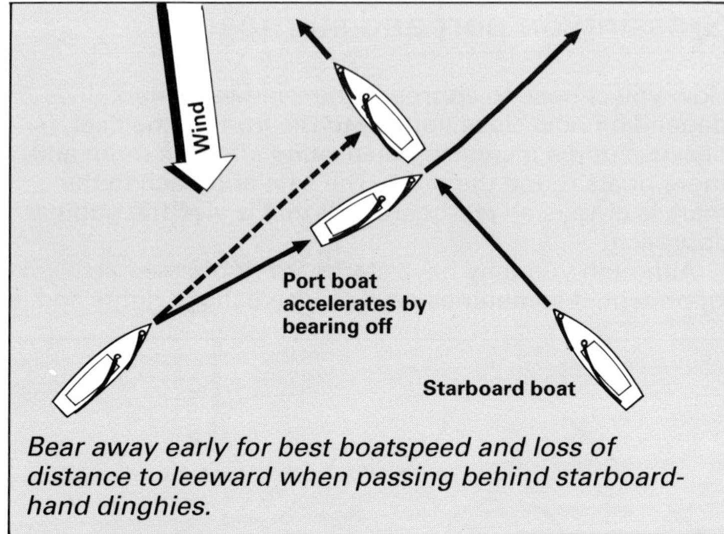

Bear away early for best boatspeed and loss of distance to leeward when passing behind starboard-hand dinghies.

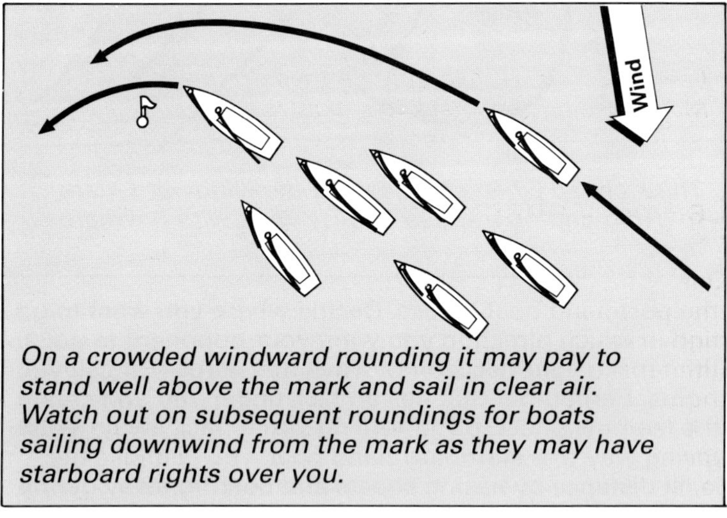

On a crowded windward rounding it may pay to stand well above the mark and sail in clear air. Watch out on subsequent roundings for boats sailing downwind from the mark as they may have starboard rights over you.

approach will give you clearer air up to the mark, and you can find a gap at the very last moment. (Read carefully Rule 41, which determines when you have completed your tack!)

When lots of boats are already rounding, usually on starboard, then it can pay to overstand the lay line on port tack, and approach still on starboard, but in clear air, going faster.

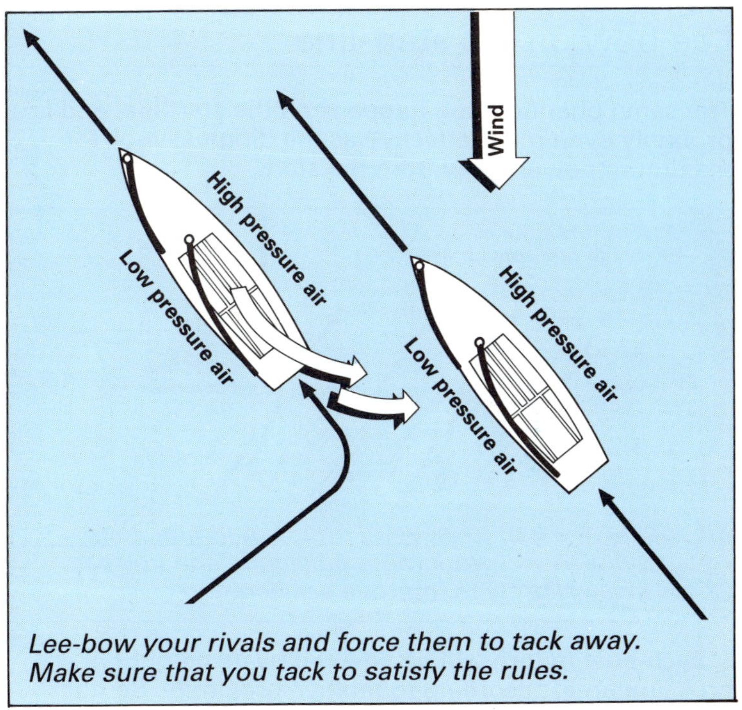

Lee-bow your rivals and force them to tack away. Make sure that you tack to satisfy the rules.

Lee-bow effect

One of the most interesting close-quarter manoeuvres is the lee-bow effect. Remember that your sailplan has a high-pressure side and a low-pressure side, and that the difference between the two is the power created to drive the boat.

If you can position yourself closely to leeward, and just ahead, then the effect of your high-pressure area will tend to fill your opponent's low-pressure area, and reduce his power. Shortly afterwards, your opponent will fall back, and begin to slide down parallel with your boat. His only course then is either to fall into your wind shadow, and drop even farther back, or to tack away into clear air. With careful planning this manoeuvre can be used to force your opponent the wrong way. The closer the boats are, the better the effect, but you must be clearly 'on the same tack' before you can force your opponent to take avoiding action.

Lee-bow on the start-line

The same phenomenon happens on the startline, and is probably even more effective as the dinghies look for maximum power away from the start.

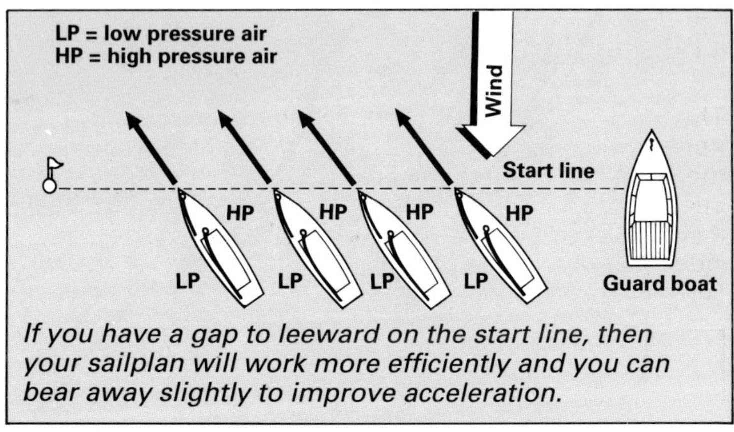

If you have a gap to leeward on the start line, then your sailplan will work more efficiently and you can bear away slightly to improve acceleration.

Each boat in turn will be affected by its neighbour's pressure area, according to relative proximity. So it is essential for good starting speed to make, or find, a gap to leeward, where no-one can affect your leeward side and reduce your power. The racing rules can help, as they

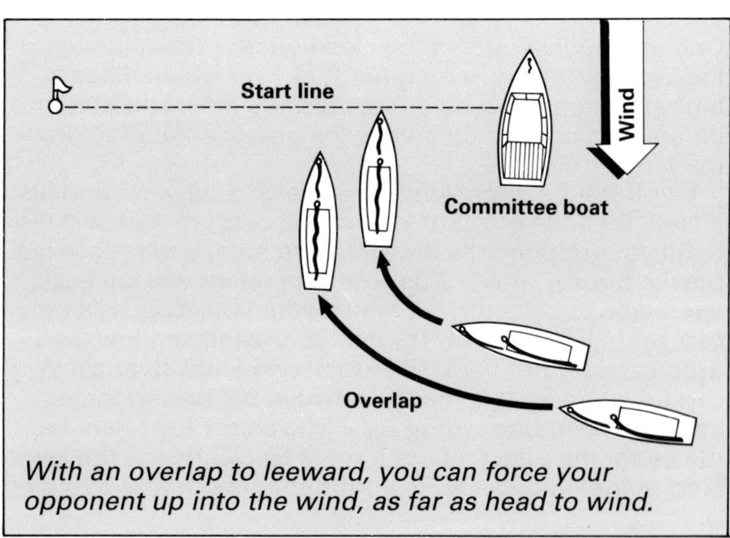

With an overlap to leeward, you can force your opponent up into the wind, as far as head to wind.

allow you to force your opponent up into the wind before the start, providing you have an overlap. (Refer to Rule 41, Changing Tack; 37, Overlap; and 38, Luffing.) You can then bear away and accelerate just before the start, whereas your opponent cannot do so until you have disappeared.

The reaching leg

The reaching legs are again decided for you by the number of boats in your vicinity. The leader should take the shortest course to the next mark, allowing for wave and tidal considerations. If the pack behind is close, then it is important to climb slightly to protect your weather side. This can lead to the whole fleet climbing above the shortest distance: the rhumb line.

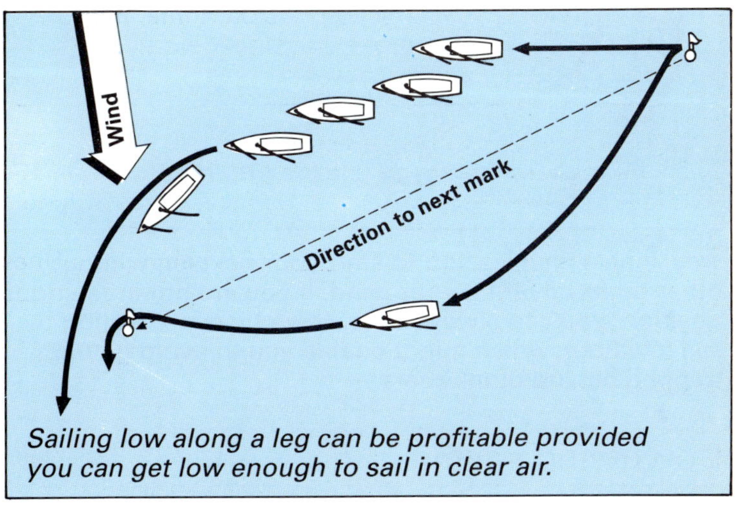

Sailing low along a leg can be profitable provided you can get low enough to sail in clear air.

Boats that climb the highest will have to sail free at the end of the leg and eventually have to run to the mark. If the fleet sails really high, perhaps getting carried away in 'luffing matches', then it is possible to sail low and approach the mark on a close reach, at speed. A good distance is needed between the boats to windward and your leeward route, otherwise you will be sailing in disturbed air.

It usually pays to be on the inside at a wing mark, because of the rules advantage which gives you right of

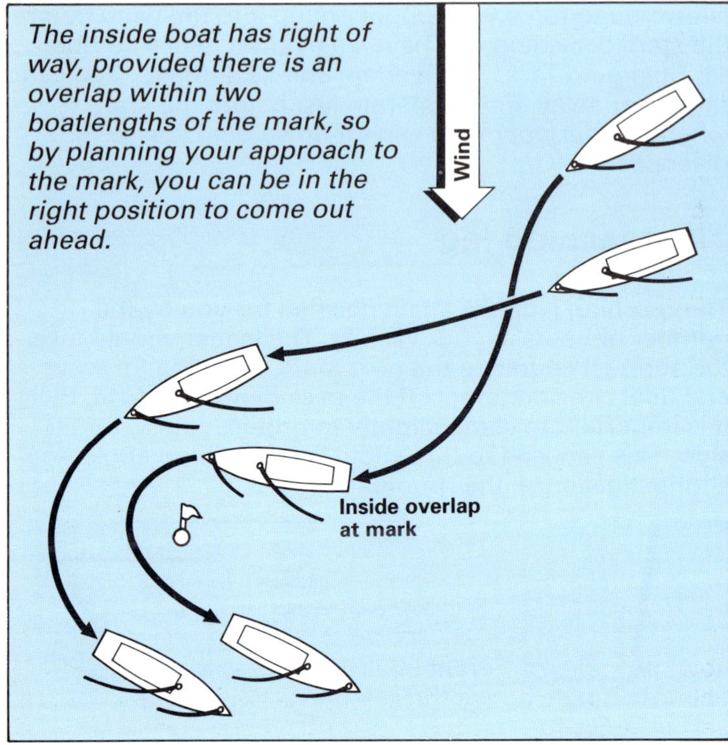

way. It also enables you to start your next leg without other boats covering your wind. If you are not in the right position, you can always slow down by oversheeting the sail (stalling), which might enable you to avoid getting trapped behind other boats.

Downwind sailing

This is very much a VMG race (see p.52), where good spinnaker handling really matters. Most boats will improve their performance by sailing a little higher than a square, dead run. The apparent windspeed and direction will change and the boatspeed will increase as the air

•**Tip** Try not to get trapped by right-of-way boats on starboard gybe — an early decision to take an opponent's transom will resolve this.

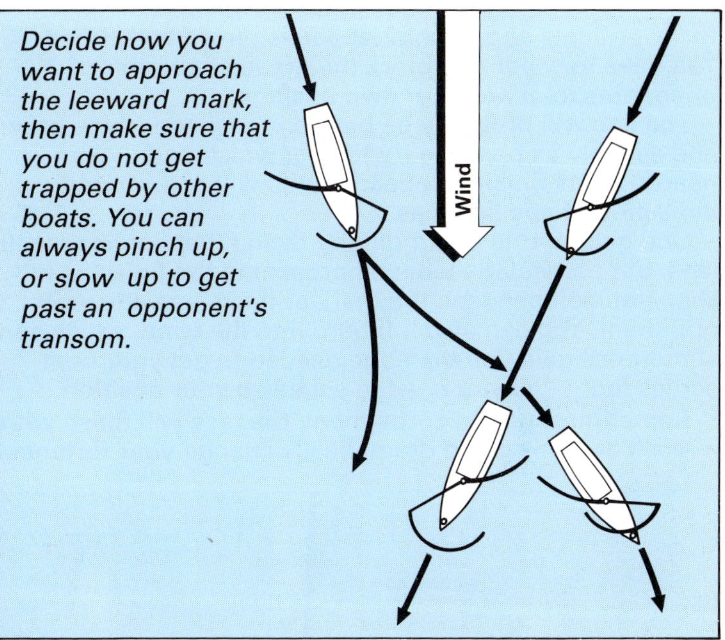

Decide how you want to approach the leeward mark, then make sure that you do not get trapped by other boats. You can always pinch up, or slow up to get past an opponent's transom.

flows. For each different boat design there will be an optimum angle above the square run which will improve performance for that given wind strength. Tactics will often be governed by tide or windshift considerations. Remember to plan ahead so that you get the approach to the leeward mark correct.

The fastest approach to a leeward mark (normally left to port) is to approach on port tack. The starboard approach gives you right of way over all port-hand boats and if executed accurately, can often gain you positions. If you are the inside boat at any mark and have overlapping rights, then you are allowed to take enough room to complete your rounding correctly, but not to force your opponents too far out. After rounding take advantage of any opportunity to tack if you need to, especially for clear air.

Approaching the finish

Over a race series it is worth fighting for every place, as they all count. Quick decision making is necessary when you are in close company, because you are often not able to cover boats approaching the finish from both sides. You have to cover and block the greatest number of opponents to guard your own position.

The line will probably be biased at one end or the other, and as early as possible try to spot which end looks nearer. Boats finishing ahead of you will give a good indication of any line bias.

One golden rule about dinghy racing that applies on all legs, but particularly when approaching the finish, is to keep yourself between the mark or finish line and your opponent. You can also luff hard into the wind, which can sometimes give you the edge needed to get your boat across first — all you need to establish your position.

Sometimes, due to curtailment, the race will finish with a reach and this could dramatically change your fortunes.

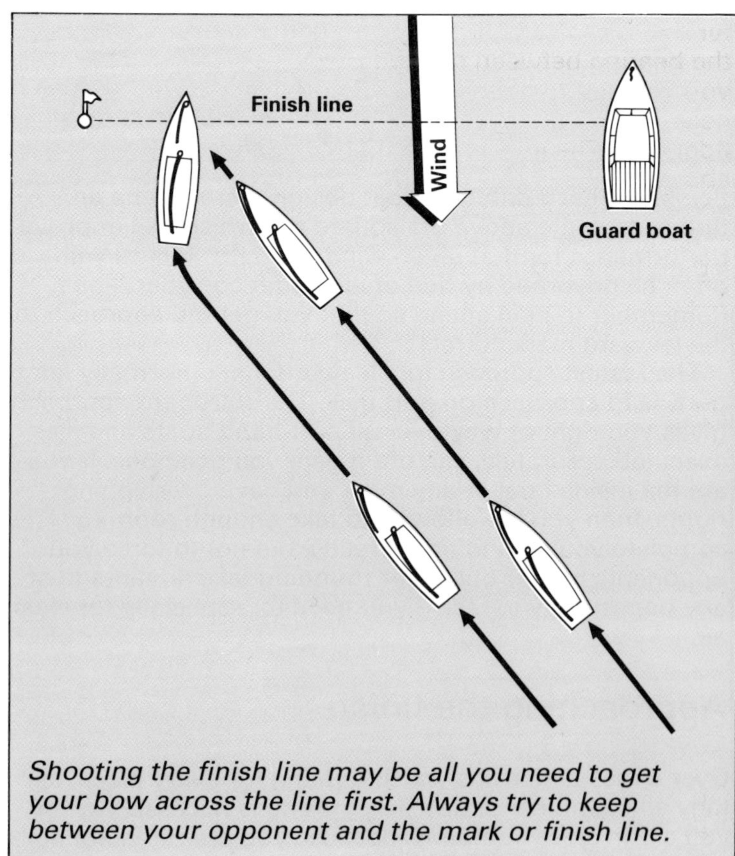

Shooting the finish line may be all you need to get your bow across the line first. Always try to keep between your opponent and the mark or finish line.

> •**Tip** Watch the way the committee boat is laying to the wind direction. This may indicate that there is cross-current, which will influence your finishing tactics.

It will probably pay to sail the course for the fastest speed, because it will not be necessary to stay up to windward.

Transits

When you are sailing along a coastline, or where there is a current, you can watch for the opportunity to take a transit, which will identify your rate of drift. Use a buoy as far out to sea as possible, and a landmark. By watching the bearing between the two marks as it changes, while you yourself remain apparently motionless, you will be able to pick up tide changes and increased strength of tidal flow. The information that you deduce from a transit about your own rate of drift can tell you whether or not you will make the next mark.

Transits can also be of help to you along the reaching leg during a race. Many sailors will be pushed higher than

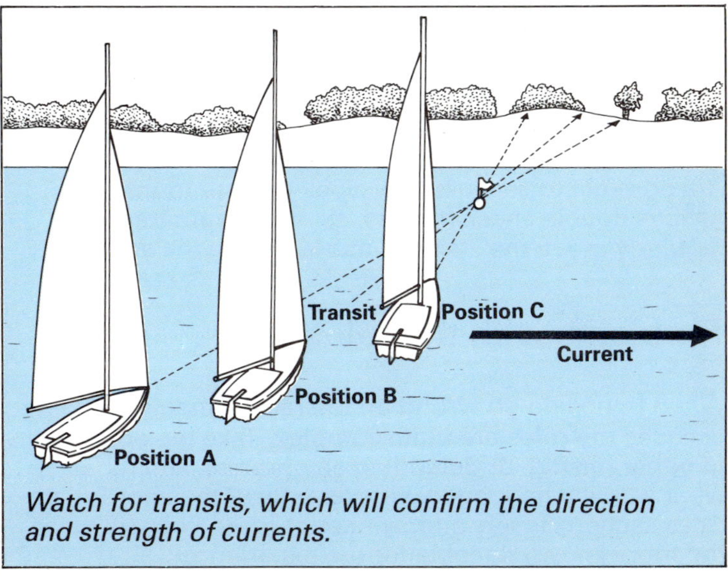

Watch for transits, which will confirm the direction and strength of currents.

the direct course, because boats ahead want to protect their windward side. This happens regularly when the tide is also lifting the fleet, and big gains can be made by sailing low, along the transit line. Look at the mark and sail a course that stops the land behind or other distant transit mark from moving.

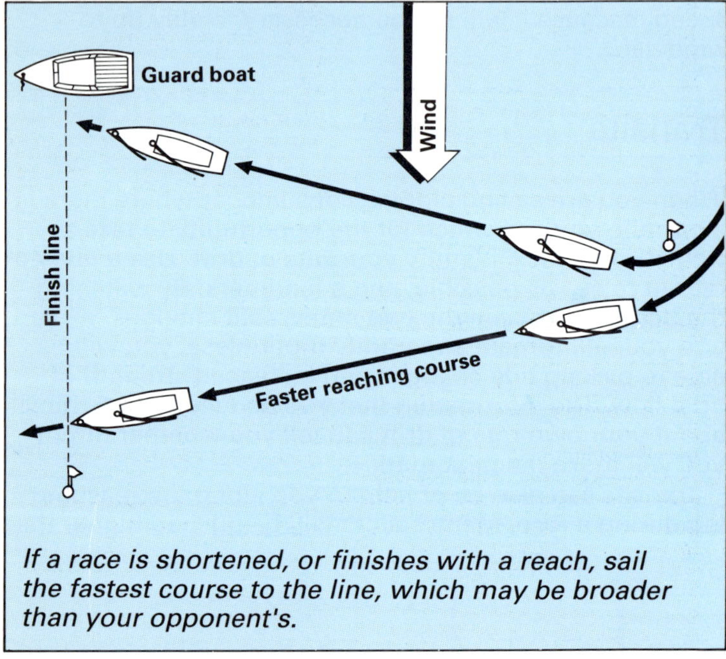

If a race is shortened, or finishes with a reach, sail the fastest course to the line, which may be broader than your opponent's.

Before a race, it is useful to check any transit along the startline, so that when you are on your final approach it is still possible to see just how close you are to the line. Always double check transits, as race committees regularly move the startline marks before the start.

Problems with the rules

When things do go wrong on the race course, stay calm, because the rules are quite complex. Take the opportunity of either raising, or defending any protest, and rehearse what actually happened with care. Read the appropriate rules section closely and, winner or loser, you will be all the more knowledgeable for the experience!

Beaufort scale

Beaufort force	General description	Windspeed in knots
0	Calm	below 1

Sea conditions
Sea is mirror-like.

Land conditions
Still; smoke rises vertically.

Beaufort force	General description	Windspeed in knots
1	Light air	1 to 3

Sea conditions
Ripples with scale-like appearance.

Land conditions
Wind direction shown.

Beaufort force	General description	Windspeed in knots
2	Light breeze	4 to 6

Sea conditions
Small wavelets. Still short, but more pronounced. Crests are glassy and do not break.

Land conditions
Wind felt on face, leaves rustle, windvane moves.

Beaufort force	General description	Windspeed in knots
3	Gentle breeze	7 to 10

Sea conditions
Large wavelets. Crests begin to break. Foam of glassy appearance. Possible scattered white horses.

Land conditions
Leaves and small twigs in motion. Wind extends light flags.

Beaufort force	General description	Windspeed in knots
4	Moderate breeze	11 to 16

Sea conditions
Small waves becoming longer; frequent white horses.

Land conditions
Raises dust and loose paper; small branches move.

Beaufort force	General description	Windspeed in knots
5	Fresh breeze	17 to 21

Sea conditions
Moderate waves, taking longer form; many white horses are formed. Chance of some spray.

Land conditions
Small trees in leaf sway. Crested wavelets form on inland waters.

Beaufort force	General description	Windspeed in knots
6	Strong breeze	22 to 27

Sea conditions
Large waves begin to form, white crests are extensive everywhere. Probably some spray.

Land conditions
Large branches in motion, whistling heard in telephone wires, umbrellas used with difficulty.

continued...